A PENGUIN SPECIAL

Where's the Justice?

Tony Gifford QC is a practising barrister and a member of the House of Lords. Throughout his legal career he has been involved in pioneering changes in the legal system. In 1970 he was co-founder of the North Kensington Law Centre, the first law centre in Britain. Since then over fifty similar centres have been set up. In 1974 he joined in starting the first barristers' chambers to be established outside the Inns of Court. The chambers are run as a fee-sharing co-operative. From 1977 to 1983 he was a committee member, and for three years, chairman, of the Legal Action Group, a law reform group now having 3,500 members. He is a member of the Labour Party in the House of Lords and a frequent speaker on Southern Africa, civil liberties and law reform. Tony Gifford is active in the field of human rights, most recently in Northern Ireland, Wales and Grenada. He has campaigned widely on issues relating to race relations, policing, prisons and the legal profession.

His other publications include *Report of the Inquiry into the Deaths of Seamus Cusack and Desmond Beattie* (1971), *South Africa's Record of International Terrorism* (1981; republished by the United Nations Special Committee on Apartheid), *Death in the Streets of Derry* (1981), *Political Policing in Wales* (1984) and *Supergrasses – The Use of Accomplice Evidence in Northern Ireland* (1984). He has also contributed numerous articles to, among others, the *Guardian* and the *New Statesman*.

TONY GIFFORD

Where's the Justice?

A Manifesto of Law Reform

Penguin Books

Penguin Books Ltd, Harmondsworth, Middlesex, England
Viking Penguin Inc., 40 West 23rd Street, New York, New York 10010, U.S.A.
Penguin Books Australia Ltd, Ringwood, Victoria, Australia
Penguin Books Canada Limited, 2801 John Street, Markham, Ontario, Canada L3R 1B4
Penguin Books (N.Z.) Ltd, 182–190 Wairau Road, Auckland 10, New Zealand

First published 1986

Made and printed in Great Britain by
Richard Clay (The Chaucer Press) Ltd, Bungay, Suffolk
Filmset in Monophoto Plantin Light

Contents

Acknowledgements

I would like to thank: members of the Wellington Street Chambers for their support, encouragement and criticism during the writing of this book; Carol Davis for her research work; Ivan Geffen, Mary Geffen, Clive Grace, John Griffith and Peter Kandler for their most constructive comments on the first draft; Helen Mary Sawyer for her perceptive vetting of the final manuscript; Geraldine Cooke for her editorial help and support; and the Legal Studies Department of Latrobe University, Melbourne, for allowing that essential time away from my practice which enabled me to get this written.

1 The Need for Justice

Few myths have been so powerfully developed by the British Establishment than that we have 'the finest legal system in the world'. According to the myth, whenever a citizen's rights are infringed there exists an array of benevolent institutions, known as courts and tribunals, which will provide a remedy. They are said to be presided over by men (nearly always men) of unquestioned impartiality and independence. To help the citizen to have access to these arbiters of truth and right, there is a hierarchy of solicitors, barristers and Queen's Counsel, whose skill, learning and devotion to their clients is incomparable.

Belief in the myth is of inestimable value to those in authority. For if this superb system of justice turns out to be constantly declaring in favour of the government against the individual, the employer against the worker, the landlord against the tenant, it means that the exercise, and the abuse, of power can be legitimated and sanctified. Once 'the law' has been proclaimed, we must all bow down and obey. Those who do not revere the courts are undermining 'the rule of law'.

The comparison with religious devotion is apposite. The practitioners of law wear strange robes – black for the lower orders, black silk for the Queen's Counsel, purple or red for the judges – and even stranger headgear. Their buildings are designed to inspire awe and reverence. Their high priests bear majestic titles: the Master of the Rolls, the Lord Chief Justice, the Lord Chancellor. To cross them, or even to protest about their decisions, may amount to 'contempt of court'. It is all designed to create an effect: respect, subservience, obedience.

Such is the myth. But what of the reality? Time after time

after time, ordinary people who become involved with the courts find that they are oppressive, forbidding, incomprehensible and unjust. They find that judges and magistrates show a constant prejudice in favour of believing police officers rather than civilians. They find that laws which they thought were passed in favour of working people become twisted against them. They find that lawyers have neither the training, nor the understanding, nor the commitment, to be effective advocates of a poor person's case. They find that people without wealth or status stand little chance in court against the big corporate or governmental institution.

The contradiction between myth and reality is profoundly disillusioning. People have a deep desire for justice. Programmes about the courts, both fictional and documentary, attract a strong interest – stimulated by the knowledge that anyone may be involved, as a member of a jury, in doing justice to others. Phrases are often used which express a feeling for justice, such as 'fair play', 'a fair crack of the whip', 'that's not cricket'. But side by side with a love of justice is a frequent distrust of lawyers and the courts. They have failed far too often to be true to those principles which a just legal system should embody.

The proposals made in this book are grounded on certain basic principles about the legal system and what it should provide:

– first, that when issues have to be decided by a court or tribunal, the people who adjudicate should be fair-minded, impartial and able to apply the law in a way that people broadly will respect;

– second, that when people have legal rights which have been violated, the legal system should provide remedies which are prompt and effective;

– third, that when individuals or groups of individuals have a legal problem which they need to resolve, they should, irrespective of their means or status, have access to legal advice and representation which is able to meet that need;

– fourth, that there are certain fundamental human rights which must be embodied in the law, and respected by the police and other authorities, if the basis of a free society is to be maintained.

These goals are simple to state and should be unobjectionable. The question is whether the British legal system achieves them. My belief that it has lamentably failed to do so derives from twenty years of working as a lawyer, and from learning over that time from those who suffer the worst injustices and receive the least legal protection: from those who are low-paid, or claim State benefits, or are badly housed; from women seeking to overcome both economic and sexual oppression; from those confronting racism, whether as immigrants or as black citizens; from people who are hounded because they are gay; and from people who have been confined by the State as prisoners, or mental patients, or children in care.

My assessment is shared by the great number of lawyers and legal workers who are part of a growing movement to secure justice for those who do not get it. The last twenty years have seen changes of enormous significance in the legal profession. In the pre-war years of the depression, and in the post-war years which saw the revolt against British colonialism, there were certainly barristers and solicitors who were prepared to commit themselves to the cause of the most oppressed, both in Britain and overseas. But they were a tiny number in an overwhelmingly conservative profession. Today there is a movement that comprises many hundreds of lawyers, and non-lawyers employed in legal offices, whose work is entirely devoted to the interests of ordinary people, particularly those who are least valued in our society. Community law centres have grown from the first one founded in 1970 to fifty-six in number in 1985. Firms of solicitors doing mainly legal aid work have proliferated. Several barristers' chambers now have a commitment to give priority service to those who are most disadvantaged. National organizations, such as the Legal Action Group, the National Council for Civil Liberties, the Child Poverty Action Group, the Joint Council for the Welfare of Immigrants and the Children's Legal Centre, have developed legal expertise and campaigning influence.

The combined experience of this movement shows that the legal system requires a complete overhaul. Instead of the authoritarian war-cry of 'law and order', a radical government needs to proclaim and implement a manifesto for justice. This book seeks to formulate some of the basic demands which such a manifesto should contain. It calls for a Minister of Justice to give the necessary political leadership and direction to a programme of reforms. It deals with the institutions which are supposed to do justice: the judiciary, the magistracy and the courts in which they sit. It examines the lawyers and the services which they provide, and the need for a national network of law centres. Finally, it deals with the protection of basic human rights, both through changes in the law and through controls over the powers of the police. In each chapter I have tried to describe the essence of what is wrong, and to suggest what must be done to put it right, with the key proposals printed in bold type. The programme presented is not utopian, but is realizable within the span of a five-year Parliament.

A book about justice and the law must recognize that the most profound injustices in our society stem from political and economic, rather than legal, causes. For example, legal rights can do little to enrich the lives of the four million people who have no jobs. If no money is spent on building new homes, then the theoretical rights of homeless people and slum dwellers are not of great value. If the opportunity for a good education and good health is a perquisite for the wealthy, then the idea of equality before the law becomes a fraud. These are the trends of the Thatcher era, and a comprehensive manifesto for a just society must include policies for reversing them all. Reforming the legal system will achieve little if it is not part of a wider crusade.

But if it is a mistake to be too naïve about policies for justice, equally it is wrong to be too defeatist. Some writers have described the repressive role of the courts, the police and other institutions of the State in terms of such fatalistic despair as to suggest that they were impossible to change. But law is an arena for political reform just as health and education have been. Legal institutions need not always, indeed do not always, represent the most reactionary values in our society. Legal knowledge, legal skills and legal remedies can be tools for change as well as tools for repression.

The government, while it cannot miraculously transform legal institutions into fountains of justice, has considerable powers to deploy: legislative powers to change unjust laws; powers to appoint and dismiss the holders of many judicial offices; and powers through its influence and leadership to encourage new attitudes of mind. Above all it has the control of public funds. Mrs Thatcher has demonstrated how a government committed to its own brand of law and order can make massive funds available to increase the pay, numbers and weaponry of the police. A government committed to justice would need to make similar increases in the budget available to the Minister of Justice. Many of the proposals in this book will cost money; but, for the sake of justice, money has to be spent.

Although there is much to be done, there is also much to build on. It is radical reform that is needed, not total overthrow. There are strengths in the system which must be recognized and preserved. There are the fundamental concepts of natural justice built into the procedures of the courts, particularly the basic rule that no one can be judged without a full hearing of the case on both sides. There is the tradition of exposing falsehood by cross-examination; while some have questioned the 'adversarial' system of justice, it should not be discarded so long as there are people in positions of power who will lie and cover up in order to stay on top. There is the Legal Aid Scheme, a major achievement in the provision of justice, which, in spite of limitations, is capable of providing a first-class and often free service to many, such as is available in few other countries.

And there is the right to trial by jury, an extraordinary inheritance from the past. Jury service is the most weighty responsibility which people are required to discharge simply by virtue of their citizenship. They discharge it with the utmost seriousness and reliability. The jury is the human face of the courts, the guarantee that those who seek to lock up their fellow-citizens cannot do so without proven and acceptable reasons.

These are good foundations on which it will be possible to build a more just legal system.

2 A Minister of Justice

The Lord Chancellor should be replaced by a Minister of Justice accountable to the House of Commons and scrutinized by a Select Committee.

The Lord Chancellor is one of the strangest persons in the British Constitution, combining in one office:

- an executive role as a member of the Cabinet and head of a government department, the Lord Chancellor's Department;
- a judicial role as a judge who may sit in any of the courts, and who in practice presides occasionally in the House of Lords, the highest appeal court in the United Kingdom, and in the Privy Council, the final appeal court for many Commonwealth countries;
- a parliamentary role as speaker of the House of Lords.

The reasons for this multipurpose office are found in a vast span of history. The first Chancellor was recorded in 1068, and a similar office was performed for centuries before that. He was the man who prepared and sent out the King's letters, and thus became the king's senior administrator. By the twelfth century he was a member of the King's Council and was hearing pleas as a judge. When the first Parliament assembled in the thirteenth century, he sat in that also. By the sixteenth century his place as Speaker of the House of Lords was established.

On every sitting day in the House of Lords, the Lord Chancellor parades through the corridors in full-bottomed wig, robe, knee-breeches and buckled shoes, sits down on the Woolsack (a seat perched uncomfortably on a bale of wool) and presides over business in which usually he has no ministerial interest. His duties as Speaker are minimal. He does not have to keep order, since the Lords order their own business. His only role is to recite the necessary form of words when questions have to be put to a decision. It is a waste of a Cabinet Minister's time.

It is one thing to perpetuate ancient rituals in order to attract the tourists. But it is not acceptable for an important government position to become encrusted by traditions which have lost their meaning. Like other areas of essential social provision, justice should be the responsibility of a minister accountable to the House of Commons, who should not necessarily be a lawyer. The Minister of Education is not required to be a teacher, nor the Minister of Health a doctor. Ministers are not meant to be professionals in their ministerial field but politicians who, with the help of expert advice, can determine the needs of the public over and above the demands of any professional lobby. Justice is no different, and the dominance of lawyers over legal policies has been a major brake upon progress towards the reform of legal institutions.

The main administrative responsibilities in the field of justice are:

- the appointment of judges and magistrates;
- the provision of courts and tribunals, and their procedures;
- publicly financed legal services, including the Legal Aid Scheme, law centres and other legal advice agencies;
- reform of the law itself.

All these need to be discharged by someone who is not steeped in the traditions of the law, who can reach beyond the conventional wisdom of conservative professionals to see what the public interest really requires.

Whether or not the House of Lords in its present form is abolished (and it certainly should be), the Minister of Justice should sit, like most other ministers, in the elected chamber. Members of the House of Commons are particularly well qualified, both through dealings with their constituents and through their work as lawmakers, to scrutinize the workings of the legal system.

A parliamentary Select Committee on Legal Affairs would increase still further the capacity of elected representatives to be involved in legal matters which have been covered in unnecessary mystery. Successive Lord Chancellors have resisted the scrutiny of a Select Committee into their field of responsibility. But all the topics in this book – the method of appointment of judges and magistrates, the quality and availability of lawyers, the complexities of court procedures, the promotion of human rights – would benefit from inquiry and debate through normal constitutional channels. The Select Committee system has served the public well in many fields, and there would be no reason to exempt the Ministry of Justice.

The Minister of Justice would not have the right to sit as a judge.

It is contradictory to the concept of an independent judiciary that a Cabinet Minister should sit in the highest courts of the land. The justification of the judicial role of the Lord Chancellor has been put by Lord Hailsham in these terms:

Because he must command the respect of the judiciary (unless some future Prime Minister should be tempted to appoint some party hack to the post, without the independence, the integrity or the necessary scholarship to defend the position) it is vital that he should submit himself to the discipline of giving, and utilize the right to give, judgment in matters of the highest importance in the House of Lords.'[1]

There are a number of fallacies in that statement. Why should the judiciary respect only a person who can deliver judgments as well as they can? It is like saying that the Minister of Defence must lead a regiment in battle before the generals will accept the minister's policies. Why should a person without 'scholarship' be assumed to be a 'party hack'? Why do 'independence' and 'integrity' depend on the capacity to be a judge? One could argue with greater force that a Cabinet Minister of integrity, who had never been a judge before, should have the humility to leave judging to the judges. Lord Gardiner did exactly that, and refused to exercise his right to be a judge when he was Lord Chancellor.

In practice Lord Chancellors have much other work to do, and sit only occasionally as judges. The law reports for 1971 to 1984 show that Lord Hailsham and Lord Elwyn-Jones presided as Lord Chancellor in a total of 29 cases out of 542, an average of 2 cases a year. So the House of Lords as an appeal court did not need them, and they hardly gained much experience in judging.

A specific duty should be imposed upon the Minister of Justice to ensure that comprehensive legal services were available to all.

The change of a minister's name does not of itself change policy; rather it should be the outward expression of a determination, which must be that of the whole government, to transform policies in a particular area of administration. Creating a Ministry of Justice would signify that the senior law minister is not just there to oversee the courts and appoint the judges, but to ensure that people can get access to justice.

At present there is no law which imposes any duty on anyone to ensure that people can get proper legal help to resolve their legal problems. There is a *laissez-faire* assumption that the private legal profession, with the help of legal aid, will deliver the required service. When it does not, as MPs and councillors find constantly in their surgeries, there is no one to complain to.

There are times when it is necessary to take stock of a recognized social need and to build a national network of agencies which is capable of meeting it. It was done for education in 1944 and for health in 1946. The National Health Service Act of 1946 made a firm declaration of ministerial responsibility:

It shall be the duty of the Minister of Health to promote the establishment in England and Wales of a comprehensive health service designed to secure improvement in the physical and mental health of the people of England and Wales, and the prevention, diagnosis and treatment of illnesses and for that purpose to provide or secure the effective provision of services . . .[2]

The time is ripe for such an approach to the provision of those services which are needed for people to obtain justice. The law which sets up the Ministry of Justice should declare the Minister's duty in terms such as these:

It shall be the duty of the Minister of Justice to promote the establishment in England and Wales of comprehensive legal services designed to secure that the people of England and Wales receive such advice and assistance as may be effective and necessary for them to obtain justice under the law for the redress of their grievances.

(I in no way intend to exclude Scotland or Northern Ireland from the scope of such reforms; but both have separate legal systems and would need to be covered by separate measures.)

Such a declaration would fix the accountability of the Minister to Parliament, and set the goal to be achieved. I deal in later chapters with the ways in which the duty would need to be fulfilled.

All responsibilities affecting the provision of justice should be brought within the Ministry of Justice.

Some of the present divisions of responsibility between the Lord Chancellor and other ministers make no sense at all. The Lord Chancellor is responsible for the administration and procedures of the civil courts, and of the Crown Court, but not of the magistrates' courts, which are the preserve of the Home Office. But the Home Secretary has major responsibilities for the police, and should be removed from any control of the magistrates' courts, in which the police have a partisan interest. For the same reason it is wrong that the reform of the criminal law is a matter for the Home Secretary, though civil law reform is for the Lord Chancellor.

The Lord Chancellor is involved, either directly or through recommendation to the Prime Minister, in the appointment of most of the people who sit in courts and tribunals – but not all. A glaring exception concerns immigration adjudicators, who hear appeals of crucial importance about people's rights to enter or stay in Britain. They are appointed by the Home Secretary, whose department is responsible for the very decisions which are being appealed against. Many of them have a background in the colonial service or the civil service. It is not surprising that there are bitter complaints about their anti-immigrant bias.

The position with regard to the funding of law centres has become chaotic. The majority have received grants from the Department of the Environment under the Urban Programme. That department has determined that it will only fund law centres over their starting years, and it expects local authorities to take over the funding. Local authorities, however, are often the other party to actions brought by law centres' clients. Many refuse to fund an agency which will sue them when they neglect their legal duties, and some law centres have had to close down after a change in the political control of a local authority. Seven law centres were rescued from closure by Lord Elwyn-Jones when he was Lord Chancellor, but Lord Hailsham, while keeping this funding going, has refused to extend it to any others. The Lord Chancellor's Advisory Committee on Legal Aid in its January 1985 report complained that 'lack of clear ministerial responsibility and direction for legal services is a chronic problem'.[3]

This confusion causes injustice, above all to those whose rights need greatest protection. What is needed is a clear and sensible division of responsibilities. On the one hand those agencies of the State which are designed to control and order people, such as the police, the prison service and the immigration service, should stay with the Home Office. On the other hand those agencies which are designed to provide justice, which includes the control of the abuses and errors of the controlling agencies, are the proper concern of a Ministry of Justice.

The Attorney-General should remain as a separate law officer, accountable to Parliament for the work of the Crown Prosecutor service.

There are two other government ministers who operate in the area of justice: the Attorney-General and the Solicitor-General. They are both barristers and Members of Parliament, the Solicitor-General being junior to the Attorney-General and assisting in the discharge of the same responsibilities, which are:

Prosecutions. The Attorney-General has to consent to prosecutions in important cases, such as those brought under the Official Secrets Act, and has the power to stop any prosecution if he thinks that the public interest requires it. He supervises the work of the Director of Public Prosecutions, and is responsible for the superintendence of the new Crown Prosecutor service introduced by the Prosecution of Offences Act 1985.

Other law enforcement. The Attorney-General is responsible for contempt of court proceedings, and has to give consent when private citizens wish to use the law on behalf of the public; for instance, a viewer seeking a court order to stop a television programme from being broadcast could not take action without the Attorney-General's permission.

Advising and representing the government. The Attorney-General is the government's senior legal adviser, and appears as the barrister representing the government when the case is thought to be really important; for example, Sir Michael Havers personally led for the prosecution in the trial of Michael Bettaney on charges of spying for the Soviet Union.

These are responsibilities which require the abilities of a trained lawyer. A radical government would need good legal advice, and good political lawyers to be its advocates in prosecuting the crimes which it had a priority to crush. For example, it would be healthy to see an Attorney-General prosecuting those who had broken a new economic sanctions law passed to help the fight against apartheid in South Africa; or to see determined law officers leading the prosecution of those accused of raping women or inciting racial hatred.

In the past both Labour and Conservative Attorneys-General have made deplorable decisions in exercising their discretion whether or not to approve a prosecution. The constitutional rule is that they must act in the public interest; in reality they have favoured the interest of the Whitehall machine. For example, Labour's Attorney-General invoked the Official Secrets Act against journalists Duncan Campbell and Crispin Aubrey, merely because they interviewed an ex-soldier and listened to his supposedly secret information. His Tory successor used the same Act against Sarah Tisdall and Clive Ponting, civil servants who felt bound by their conscience to expose evidence of Government duplicity.

The Attorney-General in a radical government would need to use the considerable powers of that office to advance the real interests of the public, if necessary against the wishes of civil servants and Crown Prosecutors. Some kinds of prosecution would have to be stopped. For example, there are many police forces who make a habit of prying into public lavatory cubicles to arrest gay men having sex. The prosecutions which follow may ruin the accused, even though they have usually harmed or offended no one. In other areas many more prosecutions are needed; for example, the Director of Public Prosecutions frequently receives clear allegations of brutality and corruption by police officers, yet hardly ever institutes a prosecution.

These responsibilities of the Attorney-General should continue as separate functions from those of the Minister of Justice. As in the case of the police, the agency responsible for prosecuting people before the courts should not be directly linked with the minister who is responsible for justice in those courts. There is sense in the constitutional convention that the Attorney-General, in exercising his powers, should act independently.

3 Judges

The Lord Chancellor possesses an enormous power of patronage. In the six years from May 1979 to April 1985, Lord Hailsham was involved, either directly or through recommendation to the Prime Minister, in appointing:

- the Lord Chief Justice, the Master of the Rolls and the President of the Family Division;
- 5 out of the 11 Lords of Appeal, who sit in the House of Lords;
- 19 out of the 21 Lords Justices, who sit in the Court of Appeal;
- 42 out of the 77 High Court judges;
- 150 out of the 373 circuit judges;
- 216 recorders and 455 assistant recorders, who are part-time judges in criminal cases;
- 30 out of the 60 stipendiary magistrates, who are magistrates with legal training sitting in London and other cities;
- a large number of full-time and part-time chairmen of the many tribunals which operate in the same way as courts in important specialist areas, such as the industrial tribunals, social security tribunals and mental health review tribunals.

These are people who exercise considerable power. They impose prison sentences and other penalties. They arbitrate in conflicts between police officers and the public, landlords and tenants, employers and employees, citizens and government. They have the power to shape the law according to their idea of what is reasonable and fair. They articulate the 'common law', which is the body of law built up by judicial precedent, in other words by the undemocratic passing into law of the judges' social and political values. When Parliament passes a law, the judges are the sole interpreters of what Parliament intended, and therefore determine how that law is to be applied. The quality of judicial appointments is of central importance to the well-being of society.

Once appointed, the senior judges have security of employment to a considerable age. High Court and Appeal Court judges may only be removed by a resolution of both Houses of Parliament, and need not retire until they are seventy-five years of age. Circuit judges may be removed by the Lord Chancellor for incapacity or misbehaviour, and need not retire until they are seventy-two.

The judges are predominantly men who have been educated at public schools and at Oxford or Cambridge universities, and have had a career at the Bar. These were the figures at April 1985 for the main categories of judges:[4]

	Total number	Men	Women	Barristers	Solicitors	Ex-public school	Ex-Oxford/ Cambridge	Average Age
Lords of Appeal and Heads of Division	16	16	0	16	0	15	15	70
Lords Justices	21	21	0	21	0	16	19	62
High Court judges	77	74	3	77	0	61	60	60
Circuit judges	373	359	14	344	29	246	235	61
Recorders	420	401	19	383	37	265	264	52
Assistant recorders	557	532	25	505	52	not available		
Stipendiary magistrates	60	55	5	40	20	42	24	54
Full-time chairmen	105	100	5	62	43	not available		
Total	1,629	1,558	71	1,448	181	–	–	57*
Percentage of total		96	4	89	11	67*	64*	–

* Figures taken in relation to the 967 people for whom information was available.

The figures in each column are alarming. If one looks at the figures for recorders and assistant recorders, the younger people who will be the senior judges of the future, one sees that the position is getting no better. The total of 71 women among 1,629 holders of judicial office is a disgrace. The number of black people is, I believe, 4.

Part of the problem lies in the catchment area for candidates. Only barristers may be appointed as High Court judges. Solicitors, though eligible since 1971 to be recorders and to be promoted from recorder to circuit judge, hold only 9 per cent of these posts – even though there are only about 5,000 barristers in total, as against about 60,000 solicitors. The barristers now in practice are likely contenders for judicial posts if they are reasonably competent and have not upset the legal establishment. The potential among solicitors is hardly tapped because, it is said, they do not want to apply, or have not enough experience in the work of the courts. A truer reason for the non-appointment of solicitors is that they are not known to the closed network of judges and senior barristers who are consulted about judicial appointments. As Lord Hailsham himself has put it: 'I give great weight to the independent views of a wide spread of members of the Bar and Bench in a position to judge a potential candidate's work and personality.' He added that this approach was being applied to solicitors 'as far as circumstances allow'.[5]

The social background of judges reflects the profession from which they are drawn. To become a barrister is very difficult for someone without private means. Socially and culturally, the Bar is a privileged profession which is structured so as to exclude those who do not fit in. So it is not surprising to find that approximately two-thirds of all the judges in the table have had a public school education and been to Oxford or Cambridge. Not surprising, but disturbing to anyone who believes that one day the judiciary should reflect the composition of the society which it serves.

What of the quality of their judging? A barrister sees many judges in twenty years of practice, so I offer a personal assessment. There are a few who are frankly unpleasant, and appear to despise the majority of those whose lives they dispose of. There are a further few who are incompetent, with little understanding of the laws which they have to administer.

On the plus side there are a number of judges who take obvious trouble to be fair and objective, so that even the loser of the case goes away feeling that the trial has been fair.

In the middle are a majority of judges who, while not being openly offensive, are affected by a deep and ingrained bias against the unprivileged individual and towards the more powerful party such as the prosecution, government department or big corporation. Sometimes the bias is quite deliberate, as when judges try to steer the jury by a mixture of comment and innuendo towards a verdict of guilty. This practice of 'putting the boot in' is commonplace, and causes great offence to those who believe that judges are meant to preside impartially while the jury determines the verdict.

Sometimes the bias is wholly unconscious, the inevitable product of judges' education and social position, and the values of their former profession. Their life as barristers has removed them further than many of their class from close contact with the working class. Consequently their ignorance of whole areas of British life is shattering. They receive no training whatever which might help them to recognize and overcome their prejudices. Their role should be to uphold the law equally and impartially; but when they have no conception of what it is like, for instance, to be a worker facing redundancy, or a woman trapped in a violent marriage, or a black youth in a police station, or a gay person in a prejudiced society, they are incapable of discharging that role. One judge who recognized the problem put the point well in a speech made in 1920, that is just as relevant to the judges of today:

The habits you are trained in, the people with whom you mix, lead to your having a certain class of ideas of such a nature that, when you have to deal with other ideas, you do not give as sound and accurate judgments as you would wish . . . It is very difficult sometimes to be sure that you have put yourself into a thoroughly impartial position between two disputants, one of your own class and one not of your class.[6]

Sometimes the attitudes of judges emerge in well-publicized political cases, when people who do not normally think about judges are startled to the point of outrage. Recent examples have been when Sarah Tisdall was jailed for six months for leaking a document which embarrassed the Government; or when the judge in the Clive Ponting trial directed the jury that the interests of the State were what the Government declared them to be; or when the banning of trade unions at the Government Communications Headquarters without discussion or consultation was held to be justified in the interests of national security; or when the Greater London Council's policy of cheap public transport fares was held to be illegal, even though the councillors had been elected to carry it out.

When dealing with the 1984–5 miners' strike, the contempt of the judges for the striking miners was scarcely concealed. One example was the ruling on bail conditions. Thousands of miners, appearing before the magistrates on petty charges, had uniform conditions of bail imposed on them, forbidding them to take part in pickets or demonstrations. Complaint was made that in doing this the courts had failed to consider each case individually. The Lord Chief Justice rejected this, saying:

By the time these defendants appeared in court, it must have been clear to everyone and to the magistrates in particular, that any suggestion of peaceful picketing was a colourable pretence and that it was a question of picketing by intimidation and threat . . . Against that background the magistrates in our judgment were right to conclude that if no condition were imposed, offences would be committed by these defendants whilst on bail.[7]

In other words, all picketing miners were criminals. By the same reasoning the High Court in another case justified the Nottinghamshire roadblock operation, in which 165,000 people (according to police figures) had been prevented from entering the county during the first six months of the strike.

The record of the judges has been fully analysed by Professor John Griffith in his book *The Politics of the Judiciary*, and I agree with his conclusion:

It is demonstrable that on every major social issue which has come before the courts during the last thirty years – concerning industrial relations, political protest, race relations, governmental secrecy, police powers, moral behaviour – the judges have supported the conventional, established and settled interests. And they have reacted strongly against challenges to those interests. This conservatism does not necessarily follow the day-to-day political policies currently associated with the party of that name. But it is a political philosophy nevertheless.[8]

In other less publicized ways, judges are constantly making choices between possible alternatives which depend entirely on their personal view of what is right, or probable, or reasonable. In cases about dismissal from a job the industrial tribunals have to decide whether the dismissal was fair 'in accordance with equity and the substantial merits of the case'. In cases where a tenant is to be evicted, the county court judges have to decide whether it is 'reasonable' to make an order for possession. Every judge who passes a prison sentence has to ask, is it necessary to send this defendant to prison? When the police are accused of extracting a confession by threats or violence, judges have to decide, do I believe the police officer or the accused?

These are decisions which cause daily injustice in courts around the country. It is most unusual for a judge to disbelieve a police officer in a direct conflict of evidence. I shall always remember the case of a Roman Catholic chaplain who had been arrested during the demonstration at Southall in West London against the National Front election meeting, in April 1979. A police officer justified the arrest by alleging that the chaplain had made violent and deliberate moves against the police line. The chaplain completely denied the allegation. I and many others in court were convinced that any reasonable court must at least be in doubt about the truth of the police version. But a stipendiary magistrate and, on appeal, an experienced circuit judge found the case proved beyond reasonable doubt. The chaplain, who had previously believed that the courts were courts of justice, was utterly bewildered. If that can happen to a chaplain, the more usual class of defendant stands little chance of being believed.

There are no quick or easy ways of altering the character of the judiciary. Judges must have a legal training, and the majority of available lawyers, both barristers and solicitors, women and men, are likely to have well-entrenched and conservative views. A Minister of Justice who was determined to do what was possible to create a more broad-based and broad-minded judiciary would need to tackle two questions: how should judges be selected, and how should they be trained?

According to the present methods of appointment, one civil servant travels around the country, talking to the judges and senior barristers in each area, asking their views on the eligible candidates. Out of these consultations emerge recommendations which the Lord Chancellor considers and approves. With the High Court and more senior appointments, similar consultations take place with various judges, with the Lord Chancellor more directly involved as the importance of the post increases. Few people outside this small circle are involved. While the Lord Chancellor, and for top posts the Prime Minister, is constitutionally responsible, in effect it is the judges who appoint the judges, and they select people of their own stamp.

The people who are selected in this way go on to the bench with virtually no preparation or training. Criminal court judges spend five days observing in a court and three days at a residential seminar. Seminars for civil and family court judges were started in October 1985. Tribunal chairmen receive no training at all. It seems to be assumed that a barrister, after ten or fifteen years in the courts, will have developed the skills and knowledge needed by a judge. But the two jobs are very different; the function of barristers is to be advocates of their clients' cases, not to make judgments about their honesty or decisions about their punishment.

The need for judges to undergo further education is particularly glaring in the field of sentencing. There are proportionately more people in prison in Britain than in any other European country except West Germany and Austria. Holland has 34 people in prison out of every 100,000 people, as against 88 in England and Wales, 97 in Scotland, and 135 in Northern Ireland.[9] There is a crisis of overcrowding in the prisons, and a wide consensus of informed opinion that too many people are being imprisoned for too long. Yet the people responsible for sentencing receive no education about criminology or about the practical experience of other countries such as Holland. They sentence on the basis of their own ill-informed notions of what is necessary to punish or deter the criminal.

The judges refuse to accept that any such education is needed. In 1981 a pilot study was carried out by the Oxford University Centre for Criminological Research. Twenty-five Crown Court judges were observed and interviewed; the study found that 'many judges appeared to have devoted little thought to the principles on which they act'. The study was intended to be the first stage of a three-year review, financed by the Home Office, of the performance of judges. But the Lord Chief Justice cancelled the whole review. According to the director of the project: 'The Lord Chief Justice told us that he did not think politicians, newspapers or the public would take any notice of our findings. The judiciary would continue to be subjected to ill-informed criticism. They were experienced at dealing with that.'[10] Such self-satisifed complacency is characteristic of the legal world.

A Judicial Training College should be established to provide a thorough education for judges in the knowledge required for their work.

It is time for Britain to move towards a professionally trained judiciary such as is normal in Europe. Those appointed to be judges would be required to spend a substantial period of study at a special training college.

There would be a mixture of courses, some general, some related to particular areas of law – crime, family, employment, etc. – so that everyone who became a judge or chairman in a specialized court or tribunal would have taken a course in that field.

There are interesting models for the education of well-educated people, such as Coombe Lodge in Bristol, which is a training centre for tertiary educators; the Tavistock Institute of Human Relations in London, where senior professionals study the relationship between those who make decisions and those who are affected by them; and the Harvard School of Business Administration in the United States for the training of senior management.

The scope of training would be far more thorough than the limited exercises at present carried out by the Judicial Studies Board. It would cover subjects such as criminology, psychology and human relations. Experts who were not judges or lawyers would play a major part, in contrast to the existing seminars which are dominated by judges. Refresher courses would be required at regular intervals. It is increasingly recognized in the world of industry that senior management needs to be trained for its responsibilities. Judges, who also carry a heavy responsibility for the lives of others, should be no less professional in their preparation for the job.

Judges should be appointed from a wide range of people, including younger people, solicitors and academic lawyers.

The development of better training would have an effect on how judges are chosen. Appointments would no longer depend on consultations with judges about a small field of barrister candidates. Men and women would be encouraged to apply for a career in the judiciary. Solicitors should be eligible for judicial posts at any level. So should academic lawyers in universities and colleges, who spend much of their time analysing the judges' judgments; many might welcome the chance of a part-time or limited-term appointment, and be very effective as judges. A change in the present requirement that a judge should have practised for at least ten years would be necessary. Appointments would, however, be subject to satisfactory completion of the training course, and reports from the college would assist in assessing the aptitude of judges for different kinds of court, and their suitability for promotion. A talented judge might become a tribunal chairman or recorder at 30, a circuit judge at 35, and be promoted to the High Court by the age of 40.

The aim must be to train and develop a younger, more professional judiciary, with the qualities which people expect from their judges: openmindedness, humanity, fairness and the necessary expertise. It will not be easy to achieve; the recognition by lawyers and judges that they have much to learn will be the first, and perhaps the most difficult, step on the road.

Judges should retire at the age of sixty-five.

There is no good reason for making a wide distinction between judges, who retire at seventy-five (circuit judges at seventy-two), and other public servants who retire at sixty-five or sixty. It is surely unsatisfactory that in all the senior judicial ranks, as the table shows, the average age is over sixty. Judges constantly have to make judgments about the fate of young people and about present-day moral, political and industrial issues. A lower age band for judges, achieved both through younger appointments and a normal retiring age, would be much in the public interest.

The appointment of the most senior judges should be approved by the Select Committee on Legal Affairs.

The Lord Chief Justice, the Master of the Rolls and the Law Lords are the high priests of the legal hierarchy, not merely interpreting the law but possessing a considerable power to change it. With some exceptions, the men who have held these offices have been pillars of the traditional establishment, men of conservative views, resistant to unorthodox ideas. This need not be. The occupants of the highest judicial offices should have the capacity to embody in their judgments the most decent aspirations of the British people; to understand that human rights are more important than obedience to past decisions; to articulate the most sensible tenets of British justice, not the most reactionary.

Indeed, there emerged quite recently in the House of Lords a liberal strand of opinion, personified particularly by Lord Scarman. He was in a minority of two to three in the case brought by the Home Office against Harriet Harman, accusing her of contempt of court for revealing to a journalist documents which had been read out in open court; and in the case of the Secretary of State for Defence against the *Guardian*, which decided that the newspaper had to hand over the memorandum leaked by Sarah Tisdall, even though to do so revealed her identity. In both cases Lord Scarman cited the European Convention on Human Rights in his strong dissenting judgments. In the Gillick case, upholding the right of doctors to give contraceptive advice to girls under sixteen, Lord Scarman was one of the three to two majority.

But after Lord Scarman's retirement, the Law Lords in the homelessness case of Mr and Mrs Puhlhofer against the Borough of Hillingdon, decided in February 1986, seemed to swing back to a heartless and legalistic approach to the law, when they declared that a family of four, living in one small room in a guest house, had 'accommodation' and so were not entitled to the protection of the Housing (Homeless Persons) Act 1977.

Such important cases, which hinge not so much on legal erudition as on the attitudes of the Law Lords involved, underline the need for more openness about potential candidates before their appointment is confirmed. The Select Committee on Legal Affairs proposed in Chapter 2 would be the appropriate forum. After completing internal consultations the Minister of Justice would submit the proposed appointee to the Select Committee for discussion and approval. It would be a valuable opportunity, before the judge assumes a powerful and virtually irremovable office, for his or her qualities to be reviewed. MPs would be briefed about previous judgments of the appointee, which will all be on public record. The Committee is likely to be very slow to veto the Minister's considered choice, but its very power to do so will emphasize that the holders of high judicial office must be acceptable to the public as well as learned in the law.

4 Magistrates

There are 26,000 magistrates in England and Wales, and all except the sixty stipendiary magistrates are lay people who need no legal qualifications, and who serve in a part-time capacity. In 1983 2,303,000 defendants were proceeded against in magistrates' courts, 95 per cent of all those accused of crimes. They imposed 35,600 sentences which involved immediate loss of liberty for the accused. In addition to their jurisdiction over crime, magistrates hear domestic cases involving the custody of children, maintenance, paternity and adoption; care cases which may result in a local authority taking children from their parents; and applications for arrests and search warrants. Under the Police and Criminal Evidence Act 1984 they have a new area of work: hearing applications by police officers for authority to detain suspects for questioning for periods of up to four days. So magistrates play an enormous part in the administration of justice. They are the face of justice which people are most likely to see.

Again the official rhetoric diverges considerably from the reality which most people experience. Lord Hailsham recently described magistrates' courts as 'people's courts', saying that: 'There is, I verily believe, no people's court on either side of the Iron Curtain or anywhere in the world which is as representative of the responsible elements in society as the lay bench of England and Wales.'[11] This begs the question, who are the responsible elements in society? The official answer is reassuring; as the Government's handbook on magistrates puts it:

The first and most important consideration in selecting Justices of the Peace is that they should be personally suitable in character, integrity and understanding for the important work which they have to perform, and that they should be generally recognized as such among those with whom they live and work.[12]

Or, as Sir Thomas Skryme, the former Secretary of Commissions (the section of the Lord Chancellor's Department responsible for magistrates' appointments), has written:

The declared policy of each Lord Chancellor since 1945 has been to make sure that each Bench is a microcosm of the local community, and this amounts to seeing that in every petty sessional division there are at least some justices from each of the principal political and social groups in the area and that the Bench is not dominated by any one group.[13]

The theory of the lay magistracy has much to commend it. Justice over everyday affairs ought not to be done by professional lawyers who may feel no identity with the greater part of the community which they serve. We have experience of such professionals in the shape of the stipendiary magistrates, who generally are allotted to the busy city courts and to long cases which lay justices cannot easily manage. With some exceptions they are case-hardened individuals who can be relied on to favour the police against the defence. Their number should be kept to a minimum.

By contrast, lay magistrates, if they were truly representative of the community in which they sit, would have many of the virtues of juries. They would be local people aware of local problems. They would have no bias for or against the police. Their decisions would carry respect and authority.

In reality the magistrates' courts are far from being people's courts, and the magistrates are no microcosm of their communities. Predominantly they are white, middle-class, middle-aged people sitting in judgment over young, working-class and often black defendants. In Michael King and Colin May's book *Black Magistrates*, the authors compare their own survey of 190 black magistrates with earlier research findings. While manual workers (skilled and unskilled) are 52 per cent of the population as a whole, the proportion of magistrates who were manual workers were:[14]

Date	Author	Sample	Proportion (%) of manual workers
1966–7	R. Hood	538 magistrates	12.0
1971–2	J. Baldwin	205 new appointees	7.5
1983	M. King and C. May	190 black magistrates	14.6

King and May also found a gross under-representation of black people on the bench when compared to the proportions of black people in the local population.

What of the quality of justice done? My own experience has been mixed. I have known benches who have listened with the utmost care and have deliberated at length, like a miniature jury, before giving their decision. But more often the impression given is of total partiality towards the prosecution. The burden of proof seems to be reversed: if the police say that you are guilty, you will be found guilty unless you can prove your innocence.

Times of stress and controversy bring out the worst in magistrates. Although their magazine *Justice of the Peace* has rightly said that 'the greater the passions, the more important the civil rights of the accused', it does not seem to happen that way. For example, the experiences of defence solicitors appearing in the courts which dealt with the 1981 inner-city riots were collated and published in the *Legal Action Group Bulletin*. These were some typical comments:

From Nottingham: The magistrates barely listened to the mitigating factors put forward, and it was quite obvious that they only wished to deal with the matter as speedily as possible. What horrified us most about the 'riot courts' was the whole atmosphere of panic among magistrates and clerks. Certainly the courts were very busy, but that is not a reason for ignoring those elements of our legal system which protect defendants, like the right to legal aid, the right to be represented, and the right to an impartial hearing.

From London: It was pure policy. The police told us that they had been informed it would happen . . . Defendants were just randomly locked up, but after a week they started coming out. What the magistrates were operating was a policy of internment.

From Liverpool: On the first day you didn't seem to get an individual hearing really. As the cases got diffused among other, liberal benches it changed. The hard benches were out that morning.[15]

Three years later, during the miners' strike, the miners experienced the same kind of treatment, with uniform conditions of bail being imposed upon batches of fifteen defendants at a time. I went to magistrates' courts in Nottinghamshire during the strike and witnessed hearings at which the hostility of the bench towards the miners and their lawyers was plainly apparent.

Few magistrates are as indiscreet as the chairman of a bench in a case in 1974, who said:

Quite the most unpleasant cases that we have to decide are those where the evidence is a direct conflict between a police officer and a member of the public. My principle in such cases has always been to believe the evidence of the police officer, and therefore we find the case proved.[16]

That verdict had to be quashed on appeal. But many magistrates think the same, to judge from their behaviour in court, and some will say so privately. Elizabeth Burney interviewed fifty-nine magistrates during a study which was published in 1979. Only a quarter expressed any criticism of the police at all. Among the majority were magistrates who expressed comments such as these:

My view of the police is that they're very much maligned. I think they're marvellous . . . Often in court they're very nice and courteous . . . I honestly don't think I've ever found a policeman who has exaggerated his case or been too tough. There must be some who do but I've never met one.[17]

Central to the quality of the lay magistracy is the system by which they are appointed. Every year the Lord Chancellor makes about 1,800 new appointments, from recommendations made by 113 advisory committees around the country. The membership of these committees is kept secret from the public. Each has around twelve members, serving for six years, also appointed by the Lord Chancellor. They are nearly all magistrates; in 1982, out of 1,900 members of the advisory committees or their sub-committees, 1,737, or 91 per cent, were serving or retired magistrates.[18]

The advisory committees advertise in the local press, write to political parties and local organizations, interview the potential candidates, and make their recommendations to the Lord Chancellor. But the real influences in the selection process hardly appear on the surface. The chairman of each committee has an effective veto, and a strong influence over the whole procedure. The secretary to the committee, usually the clerk to the justices, sifts the initial list of nominations. Political parties, the Rotary Club, the Round Table, Freemasons' lodges, the Chamber of Commerce and other organizations put up their favoured members. Magistrates themselves are a major source of nominations. Through such a process candidates who do not 'fit in', or who may be thought to have 'extreme' civil liberty views, are eased out. As Burney concluded: 'However it is played, the game of choosing magistrates, which is supposed to be aimed at diversity, ends up with a team of people more remarkable for their likenesses to one another than for their differences.'[19]

The composition of the advisory committees must be completely transformed.

If the appointing committees for magistrates consist almost entirely of magistrates, they will not produce a microcosm of society. Magistrates, particularly the more senior ones, will not see objectively how the courts in which they have sat for years are working, or what sort of people could do a better job than they do. It is almost inevitable that they will appoint people like themselves.

The way in which members of the advisory committees are themselves appointed was described by Burney in these terms:

The choice of people to serve on advisory committees, officially in the hands of the Lord Chancellor, is in practice normally left to the chairman of the committee. As one of them put it, 'membership is in the chairman's gift'.[20]

It is surely wrong that secret patronage of this kind, concerning an important area of public responsibility, should still continue.

The task of selecting acceptable magistrates is not easy, which makes it all the more important that the selecting body should comprise a wide range of people who have particular contributions to make. King and May identified various kinds of people who would be suitable members of an advisory committee:

– People who know about magistrates' courts, such as a probation officer, a solicitor who undertakes defence work, a police officer, and a magistrate from a different area.

– People who know about the local community. These would include representatives from different ages, classes and ethnic groups in the area.

– People who know about selection techniques, such as members of the Institute of Personnel Management.

The transformation of 113 advisory committees would be a difficult task, and a delicate one, for local dignity might need to be ruffled. Regional organs of the Ministry of Justice would be involved in seeking out new people. To avoid replacing one system of secret patronage with another, a model would need to be established, setting out the desired elements in each committee, the balance between them, and the bodies to be consulted in appointing them. And the membership of the committees would be made public.

The Minister of Justice should ensure that advisory committees go out to the whole community in the search for fair-minded magistrates who form a true microcosm of society.

There seems to be considerable cynicism about the appointment of magistrates. Although in theory a political balance is struck between members of the main political parties, in practice even the Labour magistrates tend to be conservative. In 1983 the Labour Committee for Criminal Justice carried out a survey of 140 constituency Labour parties to discover their experience in nominating candidates. They found that fewer names were put forward than were required to fill the expected vacancies, and commented:

The lack of names is attributable to a large extent to the sense of disillusionment which was expressed by most constituency Labour parties in their replies. The continuing lack of success and the secrecy which surrounds the selection and appointment inhibits all but the most ardent from allowing their names to go forward. Eighteen constituencies had not nominated anyone for the last three years for this very reason.[21]

The effect of such disillusionment was reflected in the comment made by one secretary of an advisory committee to King and May: 'Frankly if the Labour Party tend to make nominations at all, it tends to be of the old political hacks, round about their sixtieth birthday.'[22]

Local Labour parties are at least consulted, but other organizations do not get a chance to offer their ideas. Burney reported on the attitude of the London committee to black organizations:

The Inner London Advisory Committee merely waits for black candidates to come up through the usual channels, through party connections or through involvement in youth work for example. It is afraid to approach ethnic sources for fear of giving the impression that black justices are required to represent 'their' communities – anyone expressing such an ambition would be rejected as unsuitable for the bench.[23]

This excuse for not consulting black organizations was emphasized by King and May. They pressed the secretary of a big City committee to explain why the committee did not even write to any local Community Relations Councils. He replied:

Community Relations Councils have taken a positive lead in some areas but can hardly be said in those areas – the couple I have in mind – to be interested in the community. They are interested in a certain branch of the community. The magistracy serves the community, not a particular branch of it.[24]

What is needed is the very reverse of these narrow-minded attitudes. Members of advisory committees should be reaching out to every kind of community organization. They should be writing articles in local papers, speaking to meetings, explaining the qualities that are needed to groups who would not normally suggest names. They should be actively seeking good candidates among the unemployed, among ethnic minorities, among young people – some magistrates in their twenties would contribute some much-needed understanding of the lives of defendants in the courts, most of whom are young. They should be looking among those organizations which at present would be rejected as 'extreme', but which contain so many caring and dedicated people who would be excellent magistrates – such as peace groups, civil liberty groups, race relations groups. They should be supported by strong leadership from the Minister of Justice, in order to allay the suspicion which leads people to suppose that magistrates have to be part of 'them', the establishment, rather than coming from 'us', the community.

Magistrates should have a right to time off work for their duties, and should receive proper remuneration.

Magistrates are obliged to attend twenty-six half-day sittings per year, but the average actual attendance is much higher. They often sit on more than fifty days in a year; Burney found eight magistrates in one Outer London division who had done more than 100 sittings. The remuneration is low: a loss of earnings allowance (in 1985) of £10.50 for a half day, £21 for a full day.

All this favours the person who is leisured, or who has enough seniority at work to be able to take time off without difficulty. For wage-earning employees there is a real deterrent; people do not apply for fear of putting their job or promotion prospects at risk. There is not even a legal right to take time off for duties as a magistrate, as there is for jury service. An employee may only take time off which is 'reasonable in all the circumstances',[25] a legal provision which can be interpreted very differently by different employers. The present Secretary of Commissions wrote in 1984 that: 'A disturbing feature was the number of magistrates who have found it necessary to resign from the commission on account of their employment or because it may jeopardize their chances of new employment or retention of their present employment.'[26]

There are changes which could be made to make it easier for working people to be magistrates:

– a right to time off work for duties as a magistrate, or as a member of an advisory committee, should be written into the law;

– proper remuneration should be paid for what ought to be seen as a job done for the community, not a charitable service;

– limited terms of office of about five years should be the norm, so that people do not feel committed to a life-long tenure. After a spell out of office, people could be considered for a further term. This would also help to avoid magistrates becoming case-hardened and authoritarian after too many years of service.

There are many other questions of concern about magistrates and their courts. The training which magistrates receive is limited in amount and narrow in scope, dominated by instruction from the justices' clerks. The clerks themselves have a far too dominant influence on the decisions of many benches. Magistrates are selected, or not selected, for particular types of cases, in ways which appear not to be fortuitous. Police officers can select a favoured magistrate who can be relied on to issue a search warrant which others might refuse. A Minister of Justice who was determined to see justice done in the magistrates' courts would need to make a thorough examination of these and other criticisms which are often made. The proposals made above are only the first priorities in the development of what might one day be true 'people's courts'.

5 Juries

Among much that is cold and frightening about courts in Britain, the jury stands out as a beacon of humanity. Everyone else – judges, lawyers, clerks, ushers, prison officers – work there every day and on the whole would be happy enough to play their parts in processing people through the court and into prison, whether or not there was a jury. There was virtually no protest from lawyers or court officials when juries were removed, following Lord Diplock's report, from most criminal trials in Northern Ireland. But outside Northern Ireland the system of trial by jury remains intact in spite of many attempts to undermine it.

In my experience juries approach their task with the utmost seriousness. It was summed up for me by a young woman who had been on the jury in a trial of three Palestinians for attempted murder. The evidence against the accused had been overwhelming, but the jury had deliberated for three days before returning unanimous verdicts of guilty. She said to me much later: 'We all knew that this was probably the most important decision that any of us would make in our lives, and we were determined not to hurry it.'

The history of jury trials is a history of ordinary people whose names are not known, who have been able to demonstrate their independent integrity in the face of the power of the State. In recent years there have been many key trials, when the authorities have tried to bring intimidating charges against individuals or groups of whom they disapprove, and have been thwarted by the verdicts of juries:

– In London in 1970, and in Bristol in 1981, black activists were put on trial on charges of riot after confrontations with the police. In their defence in both cases they claimed that the police had provoked the disorder. All were acquitted.

– In 1975 fourteen pacifists, members of the British Withdrawal from Northern Ireland Campaign, were charged with 'conspiring to seduce members of Her Majesty's Forces from their duty and allegiance'. The defendants had handed out factual leaflets to soldiers, informing them of ways in which they could leave the Army if they chose not to fight in Northern Ireland. After a three-month trial, the jury took an hour to find all of them not guilty.

– In 1982 in Bradford, twelve Asian youths were accused of making and storing petrol bombs. They claimed to have been acting in defence of their community. They exposed the failure of the police to take any effective steps to deal with repeated racist attacks on Asian people. Their defence was accepted by the jury.

– In 1983 in Cardiff, four members of the Welsh Republican Socialist Party were acquitted of conspiring to cause explosions. The evidence against them depended on alleged verbal confessions, which the defendants said had been wholly fabricated.

– The Clive Ponting case in 1985 was perhaps the most resounding example in modern times of a jury refusing to observe the directions of the judge about the meaning of an unjust law. Mr Ponting had disclosed the true account of the sinking of the *General Belgrano* to Tam Dalyell, MP, and claimed to have done so in the interests of the State. The judge ruled that the interests of the State were what the government of the day declared them to be, and that Mr Ponting's defence was therefore legally unacceptable. Even so, the jury acquitted him.

– During the 1984–5 miners' strike, the police brought charges of riot and unlawful assembly against hundreds of striking miners. In contrast to the judges and magistrates, juries refused to accept that picketing miners were criminals. In every case in which these charges came to a jury's verdict, they acquitted. Then in many cases the prosecution gave up and offered no evidence, realizing that these charges would not stick.

In all these cases the authorities had been most anxious to get convictions. In all cases it is likely that a judge sitting alone would have convicted the accused. In all cases there were important issues at stake, and a victory for the authorities would have led to further repression of others not on trial.

Besides the more publicized trials, there are daily examples of the value of the jury in the British legal system. In other European countries the independent role of the examining magistrate provides considerable safeguards against errors and abuses by the police. But in Britain the same team of police officers will be responsible for investigating a crime, making arrests, interrogating the suspects and preferring charges against them. They have every interest in obtaining a conviction by fair means or foul. If the case is to be heard by a judge or a magistrate, who is likely to believe the police implicitly, the dishonest police officer has an easy task. There are many kinds of case which would almost certainly result in convictions before a judge or magistrate, but would often be thrown out by a jury. For example:

– Cases of the planting of drugs by police officers on suspects, which was a common form of harassment of black people in the 1960s. Fortunately all drug offences carry the right to jury trial, and many people were acquitted.

– Cases of gay men arrested in public lavatories. Juries frequently refuse to accept the evidence of policemen craning over cubicles to spot an act of sex; or perhaps they are simply disgusted by such a wasteful use of police time.

– Cases which depend on disputed confessions. Police officers who believe that they have the right person, but have no direct evidence on which to base a charge, have frequently resorted to promises of bail, or threats of violence, or actual violence, in order to obtain a signed confession. Or they invent a series of 'verbals' – unsigned oral admissions which the suspect never uttered. Juries, unlike judges, have frequently refused to rely on this kind of evidence.

The right to trial by jury must be defended from interference and encroachment, and extended in scope. In particular this means:

Rejecting any further limits on the right to jury trial.

In 1971 a battle was successfully fought to defeat the Government's proposal to disallow jury trial to people accused of small thefts. Now the committee on fraud trials, chaired by Lord Roskill, has recommended that 'complex' fraud cases should be tried before a judge and two assessors. This too must be resisted. The issue in fraud cases is usually whether the defendant has been dishonest, and juries are as well able to determine that in a long case as in a short one. Juries have to sit on many cases which last for weeks or even months, and are often rightly praised by judges for the intense concentration which they have devoted to their task.

Extending the right to trial by jury to people charged with assaulting a police officer.

There are many offences which are considered too minor to warrant trial by jury, and which can therefore be heard only in a magistrates' court. There is one in particular which stands out as not being minor at all: the charge of assaulting a police officer in the execution of his or her duty. The Court of Appeal has said: 'A sentence of imprisonment for an attack deliberately made upon a police officer inflicting upon him harm, however slight it may be, is never wrong in principle.'[27]

In 1983 nearly 10,000 people were convicted by magistrates for this offence, of whom 812 received immediate prison terms of up to six months. Police officers who have suffered injury often charge the suspected assailant with 'assault on police' rather than 'assault occasioning actual bodily harm', which carries the right to jury trial. It is less trouble, and they can count on the near certainty of a conviction in the magistrates' court.

Charges of assaulting a police officer can involve highly sensitive and contentious issues. They arise from arrests made in the course of political demonstrations, when important civil liberty questions may arise as to the legality of police tactics. They are sometimes preferred after the police have themselves beaten up a suspect; in order to explain the suspect's injuries, they claim that they had to forcibly restrain the suspect who was assaulting them. It is essential that such issues should be decided by a jury.

Refusing to allow the vetting of juries.

The Attorney-General issued guidelines in 1980, according to which he will authorize the vetting of juries by the police in 'certain exceptional types of case of public importance'. But the greater the importance of the case, the more sinister it is for the State to interfere with the selection of the jury. Scrutinizing the jury panel to exclude people who might be prejudiced should not be allowed to either side. Some defence lawyers want to introduce the questioning of jurors in court before the trial starts, as is done in the United States, but this could be dangerous. Both sides would claim the right to ask questions, and the prosecution, with computer-stored information at their disposal, would benefit unfairly. The names, addresses and occupations of the jurors are all that should be known. Their age and ethnic origin can be observed in court.

Defendants used to be allowed seven peremptory challenges, i.e. they could each reject seven jurors on appearance alone. In 1972 the number was reduced to three. The prosecution, however, may still reject an unlimited number. Now there are proposals from on the Government to reduce challenges still further or eliminate them altogether. They must be resisted.

There are two kinds of case where the absence of challenges would create unfairness. First, a jury selected at random can often be unbalanced; for example, there may at first be a preponderance of older people to try a youth, or of men to try a woman, or of white people to try a black defendant. After the use of challenges the final jury can be more representative. Secondly, individuals can be spotted in a jury panel who have all the appearance of having a closed or bigoted mind. There should be a limited right for defendants to reject people about whom they think, rightly or wrongly, 'I don't like the look of them'. Three challenges are entirely reasonable; the only change needed is to limit the prosecution's right to three challenges as well.

Allowing the jury to decide the case without the influence of judicial comment.

The theory is that the judge presides over a criminal trial as an impartial referee. In practice the judge acts again and again as a second prosecutor. The law allows judges to make as many comments on the evidence as they wish, provided they tell the jury that they should disregard the comments if they disagree with them. Judges start whole passages of their summing-up with words like 'Members of the jury, it is entirely a matter for you, but you may well think . . .' or 'Of course the prosecution say . . .', and then launch into a dismantling of the defence case.

No one knows how much judges influence juries; I believe that they do, although a biased summing-up will sometimes be counter-productive and provoke sympathy for the accused. Whether they are effective or not, the point is that judges should not influence juries at all. They should not express their own view and, unless a trial is particularly long and complex, they should not have to repeat the evidence at all. The jury has heard it, and yet must sit for hours listening to the judge's notes of the evidence being read back in the summing-up, with the judge's own comments added as well. It is often a great waste of valuable court time, when all that is needed is a clear explanation of the law, followed by a brief summary of the issues to be decided.

6 Courts

It is inevitable that people will feel frightened about going to a court of law. The courts lock people up, order them to pay money, decide on their rights. They are places where serious decisions have to be made. But courts do not have to be grim and unwelcoming places where the convenience of the public is largely ignored.

In the busy city magistrates' courts, hundreds of people every morning are herded through like cattle. Dozens of cases are placed on one list, all to start at 10.00 a.m. Defendants, relatives and witnesses mill about trying to discover where to go. Police officers shout out names of people who are meant to be in court. There is often nowhere to sit, let alone rooms in which to consult with a lawyer. There are no refreshments, no facilities for children. Many of the buildings are ancient and shabby to the point of squalor. Behind the scenes is the worst part: the cell area, where the defendants who are in custody sit in dingy cells, talking to their lawyers through a slit in the door or through the bars of a communal cage.

The juvenile courts are no better. Young people and their parents hang about in miserable hallways and waiting-rooms. Little is done to tell them what is happening, when their case will come on, what the procedure will be, or what their rights are. Often the case is not even started, but adjourned for a month or more. It is a poor example to set to young people who are being asked to respect the law.

For people pleading not guilty, delays awaiting trial can be terrible. In the magistrates' courts the cases of those pleading not guilty are rarely listed to last for more than a day. They then have to be adjourned, half-heard, sometimes for months, until the same magistrates can be brought together. In cases to be tried in the Crown Court there is first a delay, often of months, from the time of arrest to the time of committal for trial; then a longer delay (on average, in London, of seventeen weeks for those in custody, twenty-five weeks for those on bail[28]) between the committal and the trial. The average figures conceal many cases of people spending a year or more in custody and then being acquitted. No compensation is available to them unless they can sue the police for malicious prosecution. Usually this will be a time of great anxiety, and I have known clients who have suffered far more from the strain of waiting than from any sentence which the court would be likely to impose. The Prosecution of Offences Act 1985 contains a provision which allows maximum time limits to be set; we must wait and see when and how it is brought into force.

A Methodist minister from Liverpool wrote a devastating account in the *Legal Action Group Bulletin* of how three teenage girls were pushed through six bewildering court appearances over ten months and three different courts, before being sentenced for assaulting another girl. He concluded:

I remain one individual who has virtually no respect for the courts of this land or the decisions and sentences they dole out. I arrive at this point having followed one case through the courts. I hope that disturbs you as much as it continues to disturb me.[29]

I have heard the same views from dozens of decent people who have for the first time been confronted with the reality of the court process.

On the civil side, the county courts are meant to be the informal local courts where debts, consumer claims, housing disputes, small accidents and other claims with a value of less than £5,000 can be heard. It must be said that the county courts are considerably more civilized than the magistrates' courts, with judges and court staff often showing a high degree of courtesy and concern for the public. But there is far too much formality and legalism. The person without a lawyer is at a huge disadvantage. Lay representatives have no right to speak. Court procedures and documents are obscure. For example, one of the standard forms of summons which may be served on a tenant by a landlord seeking eviction begins:

TO THE DEFENDANT

THE PLAINTIFF CLAIMS possession of [the tenant's home] by way of enforcing a right of re-entry or forfeiture . . .

Often a person faced with an eviction order will not have attended court or appreciated the implications of the summons.

Overhauling, modernizing and humanizing the courts will be a massive task. It involves a detailed study of the procedures in the various courts; the spending of money on court buildings; and above all a change in attitude on the part of many of the people involved with the courts who do not understand, or do not care, what impression they give to the public. This chapter can only sketch out the main areas of reform, and list some particular changes which could be made without great cost or delay.

The procedures of the courts must be reshaped so that they meet the needs of the public.

In February 1985 a Civil Justice Review was announced; its objective is 'to improve the machinery of civil justice in England and Wales by means of reforms in jurisdiction, procedure and court administration, and in particular to reduce delay, cost, and complexity'. The Lord Chancellor is to direct the review with the assistance of an advisory committee of ten people, chaired by an industrialist and including representatives of the Trades Union Congress, the Citizens' Advice Bureaux and the National Consumer Council. It is a positive step, particularly as lawyers do not dominate the advisory committee.

One example of what has to be tackled in the review is the

time needed to bring an action against the police before the courts. In all the public debate about the problems of making complaints against the police it is sometimes overlooked that the law gives a first-class remedy to anyone who has been assaulted, wrongly arrested or falsely prosecuted by the police. Whereas complaints are investigated in secret by the police themselves, and rarely achieve any positive result, a civil action against the police through the court provides a full public hearing; a right in most cases to have the case decided by a jury; access to the police file of documents on the case; and, in the event of proving the case, financial compensation to the victim, which can include a punitive award of 'exemplary damages' payable to the victim by the police. In this way Mr and Mrs White, of Stoke Newington in North London, were awarded damages totalling £50,000 after being beaten up and framed by Metropolitan Police officers. However, because of the intricacies and delays in court procedures, such an action usually takes at least two or three years to bring to trial. The White case took five and a half years. Many people are not prepared to wait that long for justice; or, because of the long lapse of time, they lose a case which should have been won.

Procedure's at coroners' inquests must be changed so as to allow all parties a full opportunity to investigate the causes of an unnatural death.

Particular injustices occur at inquests, which will not be covered by the Lord Chancellor's review. Inquests ought to be a reflection of the supreme importance placed by society on human life. When life is ended in violent and unexplained circumstances, it is right that a public investigation should be held into the causes of death, with the verdict pronounced by a jury.

But while the concept of the inquest is excellent, the reality is so flawed that often the inquest serves rather to cover up the truth than to expose it. The parties are deprived of many rights which are standard in other court procedures, and the consequences are harshest for the relatives of the deceased. They have no access to the statements of witnesses interviewed by the police. They have no right to legal aid. Their lawyer may not sum up the case, or ask for a particular verdict. It is not obligatory to have a jury, and where there is one, it is virtually told by the coroner what verdict to bring in. Juries are no longer allowed even to add 'riders' to their verdicts – recommendations designed to prevent future deaths.

As a result the families and friends of many who have met violent deaths have been outraged by the ways in which inquests have whitewashed the authorities. So Liddle Towers, who was seen to have been kicked repeatedly by the eight policemen who arrested him on the night of his death, met 'an accidental death'. Blair Peach, who was killed by some weapon carried by a policeman during the Southall demonstration in April 1979, was found to have died 'by misadventure'. The coroner in the inquest into the New Cross fire, in which thirteen black youths died, took no notice of the claims by witnesses that the police investigating the case had forced and threatened them into making untrue statements. The bitterness caused by such inquests is enormous.

The inquest rules could easily be changed. Legal aid should be available to the relatives of the deceased. Documents relevant to the case should be disclosed to them. The rule which reads 'No person shall be allowed to address the coroner or the jury as to the facts' should be changed to 'Every interested person shall be entitled to address the coroner and the jury as to the facts', which would in itself secure a basic principle of justice, that every party has the right to put their case before the court which is hearing a matter which concerns them.

The jury should be accorded the same respect as in a criminal trial. If people are asked to sit, sometimes for days, to hear evidence about a tragic death, they should have the right to decide without pressure between the verdicts which the different parties ask for, and to add any rider which they think is helpful. With the help of the jury, the inquest could not only examine the cause of death, but be a life-saving exercise.

A system of family courts should be introduced for all cases concerning the family and the care of children.

The Lord Chancellor's review does not cover family cases. It will not, therefore, resolve the continuing debate over whether Britain should follow the example of many other Commonwealth jurisdictions and set up a family court.

There are two main reasons for confusion and injustice at present. First, there are two separate court systems for dealing with family disputes. The main court for obtaining a divorce is the county court, which has wide powers to deal with maintenance, the custody of children and the matrimonial home. But the magistrates' courts have an overlapping jurisdiction to make orders for maintenance, custody and other matters short of divorce. The magistrates' court procedure is plagued with delay, and the remedies available are limited; but people applying for legal aid are often told that they must go to the magistrates' court because it is 'cheaper'.

There is no sense in maintaining two court systems for the same type of case. A unified family court has been proposed by many bodies, including the Finer Committee on One-Parent Families in 1974. But there has been no response by the Government. It is said that the costs would be too heavy; but, as in so many areas of legal provision, the arguments about cost cover a lack of commitment to getting justice done.

It is time to implement the Finer proposals, which were in essence to have a two-tier structure. Local family courts would be presided over by trained judges, who would have at their disposal a skilled conciliation and welfare service. Their procedures would be as informal and unintimidating as is consistent with doing justice between conflicting parties. The judges of the Family Division of the High Court would hear appeals from the local courts and cases of particular legal complexity.

The second area of confusion, and also of great injustice, concerns the rights of parents and their children against local authorities. The law gives enormous power to local authority social workers to interfere with the family. They can obtain 'place of safety orders' to remove a child instantly into their care. They can obtain 'care orders' or (if a child has been placed voluntarily in their care) pass 'parental rights resolutions'; in both cases they then take over absolute control of the child's life. Where the child lives and goes to school, when and where (if at all) the parents can see the child, are placed within the complete discretion of the local authority.

Such powers are sometimes necessary to protect children from injury. The problem is whether their use, and abuse, are within the effective control of the courts. Again there are two quite separate systems. The juvenile courts, composed of magistrates, decide all applications for place of safety orders and care orders, and challenges to parental rights resolutions. Their powers are limited; once the care order is made, they have very little control over how it operates. For instance, if a local authority stops a mother's access to her child altogether, the mother may apply to the court. But if, as often happens, access is cut down to two or three times a year, the mother has no rights.

On a different level there is the wardship jurisdiction of the High Court. The High Court, if it agrees that a child should be a ward of court, will investigate the situation thoroughly and make any order which is required in the best interests of the child. The child will remain a ward for as long as is necessary, and its welfare will be monitored by the court. The difficulty is that when a child is in care the High Court will not accept jurisdiction, unless there is something exceptional about the case.

The rights of parents and children are too important to be left to a haphazard and often second-rate system. While magistrates, as I have argued earlier, have a valuable role to play in local justice, they remain lay people without the training which is needed to take decisions which may determine the whole future life of a child. In practice they have been far too ready to accept the local authority's case.

A family court system would provide the same flexibility and safeguards as are found in the wardship procedure. There would be judges, who would have been trained in the Judicial Training College, assisted by court welfare services. They would decide both on the initial removal of children from their parents, and on any conflicts which arise between social workers, parents and children in care. All interested parties would be able to put their case before the court. There would be a real chance of getting fair results in this difficult and sensitive area of law.

Investigations should be made to discover what useful services to the public could be introduced into existing court buildings.

The answer to shabby and overcrowded courts is not simply to build new buildings. For example, the waiting area in the Highbury Corner Juvenile Court in North London is a depressing place, even though the building is modern. Humanity and concern can provide an environment of justice, even in buildings which ought to be pulled down. Ideas which are feasible would include:

– Printing notices and leaflets which tell people about the court and its procedure, and explain what rights and facilities were available to them.

– Getting cases listed at stated times through the day so that people's time and lawyers' costs are not wasted by endless hanging about. In a busy magistrates' court, up to 100 cases may be in the list, all due for hearing at 10.00 a.m. A solicitor once timed his waiting periods over four weeks, and found that he had spent 29 hours waiting in order to spend 6 hours in court, an average of $1\frac{1}{2}$ hours wait each day for a court appearance of $11\frac{1}{2}$ minutes.[30]

– Providing crèches or play areas: even the bigger courts make no provision for women with babies or young children.

– Providing chairs to sit on. Some courts have nothing but a long, hard bench in the court foyer. A modicum of imagination and money could provide more civilized seating arrangements.

– Providing magazines to read, particularly in the juvenile courts where young people get bored and fed up as they wait for their cases.

– Providing refreshments. In the larger courts there are canteens, and in some others the Women's Royal Voluntary Service provides hot drinks. But even where there is no space and no WRVS, a machine at least could be installed. Waiting for a case is tense, and a cup of tea helps.

These and other ideas would be likely to emerge if those who used the courts, such as solicitors, law centre workers, probation officers and police officers, were seriously consulted about possible improvements. The Ministry of Justice would initiate and co-ordinate the necessary investigations.

Court officials, and not the police, should be responsible for arranging business in the magistrates' courts.

Magistrates' courts used to be called police courts, and although the name has changed, the reality in many courts has not. The commanding figure in a busy magistrates' court is the dock officer, who calls out the cases, decides in what order they should be heard, and marshals people in and out of the dock. Outside in the corridors other police officers are calling out names and checking defendants against the court lists.

The police should have no part in the running of a court. They are parties before the court, which should be administered by officials who are independent of the parties. The jobs done by the dock officer should be, and in some courts are, done by the court ushers under the supervision of the court clerk. Police may be needed to help keep order or to stop people from escaping, but they can be there silently for that purpose, not as a vocal and threatening part of the court machinery.

The dock should be removed from the courtroom.

Inside every criminal court, the dock is a central feature. People accused must stand there, conspicuous and isolated. The law may presume them innocent, but in the dock they are made to look, and to feel, very guilty indeed. In addition the dock makes communication between lawyers and their clients difficult to the point of absurdity. The dock is often at the back of the court, with rows of seats between defendant and barrister. If the defendant has had the foresight to bring pen and paper, messages get passed from the defendant to the prison officer in the dock, and then to the usher, to the solicitor's clerk, and finally to the barrister. If a point arises on which the barrister needs information, the solicitor's clerk has to scurry off, speak to the defendant, and relay the answer back.

Why cannot people on trial sit next to, or just behind, their barrister? Security is not the main reason, for the dock is used in every case, even if the defendant has been on bail. The real reason lies in the attitudes of those involved with the law. They choose to isolate, and thus to degrade, the accused. Many barristers keep even their own clients at a distance. It would not be difficult to stipulate that the dock should not be used unless security plainly required it. In time it should be eliminated as a physical feature in the courtroom.

Competent interpreters must be provided by the courts.

The provision made in the courts for people who speak no

English is inadequate. Often it is left to the police or the defence solicitor to find an interpreter. Sometimes the court officials obtain one from lists which they keep, but there is no system for ensuring that interpreters are competent or have any knowledge of legal procedures.

The most scandalous case which came to light recently was that of Iqbal Begum, who had pleaded guilty to murdering her husband, even though she had been greatly provoked by her husband's violence and had an obvious defence to the murder charge. She spoke only Urdu, but her interpreter was a Gujerati speaker who knew little Urdu and spoke to her in Hindi. He was an accountant, a former client of Iqbal Begum's solicitor; quite apart from language problems, he knew nothing of the difficult legal concepts of murder and manslaughter. The lawyers complained that their client would hardly speak to them, without bothering to find out why. The case of Iqbal Begum, who spent four years in prison before her conviction for murder was quashed by the Court of Appeal, should by itself cause a thorough inquiry into court interpreting.

Lay representatives should have the right to speak in the county court and magistrates' courts.

People are often overawed and tongue-tied in a courtroom. They are entitled to represent themselves, but often cannot do justice to their case. They are allowed to have a friend to sit by them and give them advice, but only lawyers may speak for them. Often a case will not qualify for legal aid for a lawyer, but there are important points which a lay adviser could make, for example in cases about the payment of rent arrears or fines.

Some judges allow community workers, or tenants' representatives, or law centre workers who are not lawyers, to speak in court. Others stick by the strict rules, and in the magistrates' courts lay representatives are not heard at all. In an adversarial system the court needs all the help and information it can get in order to do justice. Lay representatives have played an important role in tribunals, where anyone may act as representative, and they should not be excluded from the courts.

7 Barristers

Members of the public depend on barristers and solicitors to obtain legal advice and redress for their grievances. They also pay a substantial proportion of the incomes of many lawyers; for instance, approximately 50 per cent of the fees of barristers are provided from public funds.[31] So the public, and the government on its behalf, has a legitimate interest in the quality of the service which lawyers provide.

Both as consumers and taxpayers, the public is entitled to expect the legal profession to conform to some basic standards:

– First, the right to practise as a lawyer should not depend on privilege or wealth but on ability. The most able people are needed from every kind of background.

– Second, lawyers should be knowledgeable in the law. This means both that lawyers should have received a basic training, through academic work and in-service experience, in the theory and practice of law; and that those who claim to offer specialist skills should have qualifications on which to base that claim.

– Third, the client of a lawyer is entitled to expect a basic commitment of the lawyer to the client's cause. Being a lawyer means being a person's representative and advocate. It means upholding the interests of the client to the limit which the law allows, in circumstances which are often anxious and stressful. A frequent complaint which I have heard about lawyers is that 'my lawyer doesn't seem to care about my case'. When that happens there has been a failure of commitment, or of communication, or both.

The Bar is meant to be the specialist branch of the legal profession. Like consultants in medicine, barristers are retained only through the agency of other practitioners, the solicitors. They number only 5,000, as against 60,000 solicitors. Their advice is decisive in many cases. In a difficult case a client may only get legal aid subject to a favourable counsel's opinion; or may have the legal aid revoked if the barrister considers that the case should be settled out of court. In the criminal courts a barrister's advice to plead guilty can put considerable pressure upon a frightened, but perhaps innocent, defendant. For example, many barristers in 1985 advised miners to plead guilty to unlawful assembly. Some did so and went to prison. Others were able later to change their plea and be acquitted, when the prosecution decided to offer no evidence against them.

Moreover barristers have a number of exclusive rights. They alone may appear as advocates in the High Court, the appellate courts and (with minor exceptions) the Crown Court. They have reserved to themselves all the most senior judicial appointments. They maintain a kind of elite within an elite – the Queen's Counsel, appointed each year by the Lord Chancellor, who occupy special seats in court, wear special dress and receive specially high fees.

There are indeed a number of barristers who deserve the status of specialist. There are experts both in particular fields of law, and in the techniques of advocacy. They are available to the solicitors whose clients have more complex problems than the solicitor can resolve. They can appear in long trials which most solicitors would not have the time or inclination to take on. Any reforms in the system must preserve the availability of such specialists.

Nevertheless the Bar as a whole has failed to meet those three basic standards expected of a sound public service. Its failure can be seen in the education and training which barristers receive; in the way in which recruits to the profession are selected; and in the service which is given by large numbers of its members.

Most barristers and solicitors start their legal education with a law degree. But the law courses at most universities and polytechnics are narrow in their scope, their syllabuses geared to the demands of the professions. Students learn about law as a set of rules laid down by statutes and judicial procedures. They learn little or nothing about the purpose of law, nor about human rights, nor about other systems of law, nor about the economic and social context in which law has developed. From the start the study of law has little to do with the pursuit of justice.

After the degree course the paths of would-be barristers and would-be solicitors separate. Those intending to be solicitors take a one-year vocational course ending in a Final Examination, followed by two years of articles – salaried, in-service training in a solicitor's office. Intending barristers take a different one-year Final Examination course, available only in London, followed by one year of pupillage – unpaid time observing another barrister at work. In addition they have to undergo the absurd and costly ritual of eating thirty-six dinners in the dining-hall of one of the Inns of Court.

In any other field the specialist would undergo general training and experience before progressing to a specialist qualification. In the law the position is topsy-turvy: the 'specialist' qualifies in a *shorter* time than the general practitioner. A solicitor may represent a client in court (and then only a lower court) after completing all stages of training (law degree plus three years). A barrister may appear in *any* court after six months of pupillage (law degree plus one and a half years). Furthermore the barrister has missed out on all the valuable experiences of work in a solicitor's office, such as interviewing clients, negotiating, dealing with legal aid and court forms. The 'specialists' are often inexperienced young people trying to learn a difficult job, without supervision, at the expense of their clients.

Even more shameful is the Bar's perpetuation of a career structure which discriminates heavily in favour of those with wealth and connections. Whereas articled clerks receive a wage (though the minimum of £3,500 is too low), pupils do not. There are a few scholarships offered by the Inns of Court, and some 'pupillage awards' given by sets of chambers. These averaged £875 for six months in 1985, and only 27 per cent of barristers' chambers offered them at all. Newly qualified barristers also have heavy costs, in addition to the expense of living: £232 to buy a wig and gown; £75 fee to the Inn of Court to be called to the Bar; and the costs of dark suits, travel to court, books, etc. Many first-class law students rule out a career at the Bar because they simply cannot afford it.

The literature given to intending barristers contains signs of the elitist life which is expected of them. Describing the Inns of Court, the guidance notes issued by the Council of Legal Education say:

The Inns are 'colleges' of barristers dating back to medieval times and each one has its own great history and tradition. Students share in a 'collegiate' life with the 'Benchers' (i.e. Masters of the Bench, the governing body of the Inn – usually Judges or eminent counsel) and the practising barristers of the Inn, and a student's loyalty throughout his or her life is to the Inn. Choosing an Inn is largely a matter of personal preference. The Inns rank equally with one another, and choice is often influenced by sentiment or family association, or such considerations as the valuable prizes and scholarships which each Inn offers.

The student who looked on from there to the brochure about Middle Temple scholarships would find that out of thirty-five scholarships, ten were reserved for 'male members of Oxford or Cambridge University'.

At the end of pupillage the barrister must find a 'seat in chambers', without which he or she cannot become established at the Bar. Vacancies for these precious seats are rarely advertised. They are allocated to those who fit in, who are there as pupils at the right time, and who are favoured by the chambers' clerk. Women and black barristers suffer gross discrimination. Many able barristers hang on for as long as they can afford to wait, then are forced into jobs elsewhere. Many undistinguished products of the right university are preferred. It is a lottery, with the well-off and the well-connected having favoured tickets in the draw.

A sense of what this archaic form of training is like can be gathered from remarks made to me recently at a meeting with a group of pupils:

'You're a dogsbody – the barristers have no time to really teach you.'

'You make the tea and take it round, but you're not allowed to drink it with them.'

'It's arbitrary luck whether you get in. It's very demoralizing – you constantly think about leaving. You're living on the breadline. But for people with money it's all well and good.'

'I was asked, didn't I think it would be embarrassing for my clients if I was briefed.' (a black pupil)

'I was told that the head of chambers would not take a female – it would be over his dead body.'

'I was asked in my interview whether I was going out seriously with a man.'

At an annual meeting of the Bar I once explained that this system could easily be changed. In our chambers in Wellington Street, Covent Garden, all pupils are paid from the start, receiving £6,825 in their first year. We advertise vacancies and interview thoroughly to find the best candidates. We offer the security of a place in the chambers to all pupils if they are good enough. We have in this way trained over a dozen barristers, many of whom could not otherwise have afforded a career at the Bar. The meeting listened in silence, and two judges urged other chambers to adopt the 'Gifford scheme'. But no set of chambers has come anywhere near this level of pupil remuneration.

What of the service provided by those who make it into the Bar? The best are real experts, very skilled in the art of persuasion, tough and effective in cross-examination. But there are hundreds of others, at all levels, whose commitment to their clients, particularly if they are legally aided, is superficial. They will often receive a brief only on the night before the hearing of the case; spend a rushed, tense half hour with the client before the case is called on; treat his or her problem with disdain (another mugger, shoplifter, demonstrator, or whatever); fail inevitably to grasp the human realities of the client's situation; and end up speaking in court in a manner which carries little conviction.

I know this goes on. I have seen it again and again. I have heard the smug talk in the robing-rooms. I know many solicitors, particularly outside London, who are in despair at the lack of even a handful of local barristers who are prepared to fight the case of a working-class client as if they believed that it was important and true.

Few people outside the legal system appreciate that if you are appearing before the Crown Court, which means that you will have been charged with a serious offence, you are most unlikely to meet the barrister who is to speak for you before the morning of the trial. In a survey done in 1976 in Sheffield, 96 per cent of defendants pleading guilty and 79 per cent of those pleading not guilty had never met their barrister before the day of the trial.[32] The theory is that the solicitor will have instructed the barrister in everything that is relevant, and that any barrister is competent to take the written instructions and speak to them in court.

In my experience this approach leads to a shoddy service. Advocacy is far more than rehashing a written brief. It is winning the trust and confidence of the client, understanding his or her individuality, delving into the details of his or her experience, avoiding the easy stereotype, in order to present to the court a case which is real, believable, persuasive, a true reflection of what the client would wish to say.

It is important to recognize that an institution like the Bar cannot be changed overnight. One is tempted to put forward utopian reforms of the education, training and organization of barristers, which would never be carried out because the barristers would refuse to co-operate. As in many other parts of the legal system, a change of attitude is needed, not just a change in the rules. However, there are some reforms which a government could directly undertake.

All qualified lawyers should be given rights of audience before all courts.

The artificial rules about rights of audience contribute much to the alienation between lawyer and client. However simple your case, however experienced your solicitor, you are required by law to have a barrister if your case happens to be in one of the courts in which the Bar has exclusive rights of audience. The case of Cyril Smith, MP, who wished his solicitor to read out in court an agreed statement in settlement of a libel action, but who was forced to retain a barrister to do it, served to highlight the absurd and expensive consequences of the present rules. Any trade union leaders seeking to maintain such a restrictive practice would be pilloried with accusations of overmanning and the feather-bedding of their members' jobs. But the Bar continues to assert that the abolition of these exclusive rights would spell the end of the specialist barrister and be against the public interest.

The simple laws of supply and demand make nonsense of this argument. If the public needs specialist barristers, as for many purposes it does, then specialist barristers will remain in business to supply that need, and need no protection from a monopolistic rule. There are already many types of case where solicitors have rights of audience, but barristers are regularly used:

– At planning inquiries anyone, whether solicitor or barrister or lay person, may represent an interested party. Yet there is a flourishing planning bar. Big institutions are commonly represented by barristers, but solicitors appear as and when it is thought appropriate. The needs of the client prevail, not an arbitrary rule.

– In the Employment Appeal Tribunal, rights of audience are available to any legal or lay representative. The bar has not been squeezed out: in 100 cases from the law reports for 1983–4, barristers appeared for 72 per cent of the employers and 63 per cent of the employees.

– In county and magistrates' courts solicitors do most of the advocacy, but barristers are used, especially in cases which are long or complex, where the needs of the client make it sensible to retain them.

Lawyers in Victoria, South Australia, Western Australia and New Zealand operate within the same tradition as in Britain, but find no need for exclusive rights for barristers. They qualify through a single examination to be 'barristers and solicitors', possessing rights of audience in every court. Thereafter a lawyer may at any stage choose to become a barrister, accepting cases only from other lawyers. The flexibility works well; some barrister–solicitors have become experienced advocates, but most of the higher court work is handled by barristers.

The immediate effect of abolishing the barristers' monopoly would be slight. Virtually every case in the House of Lords and the Court of Appeal would stay with barristers, as well as most in the High Court and the Crown Court. Most solicitors would not want suddenly to take on a lot of advocacy work.

Over time, a sorting out of options would take place. Some solicitors would extend their advocacy practice from the magistrates' court into the Crown Court, particularly on short cases. Barristers would have to sharpen up their service; they would be less likely to switch briefs from barrister to barrister, if the solicitor had the option of doing the case personally. Some firms would employ in-house advocates, but the independent barrister would still be valued. Many good barristers would remain as barristers in preference to a safer, but less attractive, partnership with a firm.

Too often the argument has been conducted in terms of the 'fusion' of solicitors and barristers, as if the only choice were between rigid demarcation on the one hand, and turning every lawyer into a composite all-purpose non-specialist on the other. The Royal Commission on Legal Services fell into this error, concluding that fusion would 'disperse the specialist service provided by the Bar'. But the Royal Commission accepted that the system operated in Australia and New Zealand works well. If monopoly rights were removed from the English Bar, the barristers would get a blast of healthy competitive fresh air; the solicitors would have the option of extending their range of service; and the public would be the overall winner.

The Minister of Justice should require the Bar to elaborate a fair system of recruitment.

Ideally the separate entry arrangements for the Bar should be abolished altogether, so that every prospective lawyer would qualify as a barrister and solicitor after an examination course and a period of in-service training. As in Australia and New Zealand, those who wanted to specialize as advocates could be admitted to the Bar at any time after qualification, subject perhaps to taking an advocacy training course. Instead of the present arrangements which require law students to choose what sort of lawyer to be before having any experience on which to base an informed choice, the decision to be a barrister could be made in the light of a lawyer's own experience of advocacy work, and awareness of his or her own aptitudes.

However, for a government to impose this directly would require a major interference with legal education and training, areas which so far have been left to the lawyers to regulate. Is this necessary? Yes, unless the Bar authorities are prepared to make radical changes in their own procedures.

There are signs that the leaders of the Bar are beginning to appreciate that there are problems to be resolved. They are aware that solicitors' firms are recruiting good law graduates by offering them a tempting starting salary. They have set up a committee to inquire how the quality of entry to the Bar can be improved. They have extended the number of pupillage awards and loan schemes which are available. They have recognized the existence of racism in their profession, and have made it a specific disciplinary offence to be racially discriminatory in the selection of pupils or new members of chambers.

But these are only tiptoeing steps into the modern world, and the Bar needs pushing much harder. It is simply not acceptable that such an important profession should require its future members to pay their way on to a place on the career ladder. It is as outrageous as was the practice of purchasing commissions in the nineteenth-century Army. Our chambers have shown that fair and adequately paid procedures for the training and recruitment of new members are possible. If the Bar will not introduce something similar, using its considerable resources to levy the requisite funds to pay pupils, it should not complain if the government eventually has to intervene.

The status of Queen's Counsel should be abolished.

It is odd that a profession which prides itself on being independent of government should permit a government minister to confer honorific accolades upon its senior members. To become a Queen's Counsel, a barrister need pass no examination, write no thesis, undergo no interview. He or she submits an application to the Lord Chancellor, who consults with senior judges and decides whether the applicant is worthy of the honour. There is no parallel in any other walk of life. Becoming a Queen's Counsel gives barristers no rights which they did not have before, though it does considerably enhance the fees which they can charge.

A justification for this was put forward to the Royal Commission by the Society of Labour Lawyers, and accepted in the Royal Commission's report: 'The rank of silk is not merely an honour for those who acquire it. It is beneficial to solicitors and their clients to be able to identify the top men in their profession.'[33]

Leaving aside the sexist language, the proposition advanced here is curious. The leading people in any profession become known by their reputation, and solicitors working within the law should not need the Lord Chancellor to identify them. Legal life could function perfectly well without Queen's Counsel. When cases need two barristers – and many do – solicitors should be capable of choosing. In criminal cases many solicitors are now briefing a good 'junior' to lead a difficult defence. It is much better for lawyers to be assessed by their talents and reputation, not by the bestowal of an honour by the government.

Wigs and gowns should no longer be worn by barristers and judges.

Getting rid of wigs and gowns is an important reform. It is not just that wigs are uncomfortable, hot in summer, ridiculous to look at, and especially absurd in requiring women to appear in the headgear of eighteenth-century gentlemen. The wig and gown are intended to convey a message: that we, judges and barristers, are different and superior; that we have more in common with each other than with you, the litigants; that we practise a craft which you can never understand. I am always very conscious of the effect of a wig on clients; I tell them that I have to put on this fancy-dress, and reassure them that I have not stopped being on their side.

For lawyers and judges to wear ordinary suits would not in itself remove oppression from the courts. But it would be one step which would indicate that we were working to create a modern, human, sensible court system.

8 Solicitors

For centuries the role of lawyers in our society was clear and unquestioned, at least by the lawyers. It was to advance the interests of the propertied classes. Whole areas of the law were developed for no other purpose than to maintain property securely in privileged hands. Laws about tenure of land gave absolute power to the landlord over the tenant. Laws about trusts and settlements ensured that wealth passed down the family line. Laws of contract upheld the sanctity of a 'bargain' irrespective of the pressures upon the poorer party. The criminal law visited upon the dissenting masses a variety of dire penalties for crimes such as 'conspiracy' and 'unlawful assembly', if they should join together to challenge the power of the few.

Such a powerful legal armoury needed skilful technicians. A parasitical legal profession developed in order to minister, at great profit to themselves, to the needs of the wealthy. The idea that poor people might need lawyers entered at best as a charitable afterthought into the legal mind, in the form of 'poor men's lawyers' and 'poor person's committees'. As the Royal Commission on Legal Services put it:

The characteristic of all measures for representation of poor people until the end of the Second World War was either that they required lawyers to act as a matter of charity without making a charge, or that the fees that might be paid (often on a fixed scale) were inadequate and involved working at a loss.[34]

In 1949 the Legal Aid and Advice Act was passed. It was a radical measure. It was based on the principle that no one should be prevented from obtaining the services of a lawyer through lack of means. If a litigant had an arguable case, State funds would be available, subject to a means test, to enable him or her to be properly advised and represented. This was not to be a second-class service. People would be able to choose their solicitors and barristers, who would act for them as for a private client, but the bills would be discharged by the State through the Legal Aid Scheme. The Scheme at its start in 1950 covered about 80 per cent of the population, some paying a contribution to their legal costs, some getting a wholly free service.

That this was a genuinely progressive measure is borne out by a comparison with most other Western countries. In Britain it is possible for a barrister and (with much harder work) a solicitor to make a living entirely from legally aided cases. In the United States and in most countries of Western Europe this would be out of the question. They have salaried public defenders and lawyers assigned to poor people's cases; but in general the client must either find the money for the lawyer's fees, or find a lawyer who is sufficiently committed to do it for nothing, either in the hope of a contingency fee or through subsidizing the case from other earnings.

For all that the solicitors' branch of the profession has changed little. They have not moved in great numbers to address the problems of the ordinary wage-earner. Only 4 per cent of solicitors' firms receive more than 40 per cent of their gross income from legal aid.[35] Whereas every family, since the introduction of the National Health Service, registers with a doctor as a matter of course, only a minority of people would naturally consult a solicitor over a legal problem. Many who do approach solicitors find that if they undertake work under the Legal Aid Scheme at all, the service provided is skimpy and ill informed. Often a junior clerk will handle the legal aid work, while the partners deal with the business clientele. Barristers who do legal aid work have plenty of experience of ill-prepared briefs received from many solicitors' firms, who have not appeared to understand, or bothered to follow up, essential aspects of the client's case.

In the report of the Royal Commission there is this assessment of the adequacy of legal services:

The need for legal services may be estimated in a number of ways but its extent cannot be precisely quantified. The evidence before us is nevertheless clear that, however restricted is the definition of need for legal services, *such services are, in some areas and for certain classes of society, not available*. In respect of some types of business, there is no complaint. The evidence received from industrial and commercial interests shows that their needs are met and they are for the most part well satisfied with the service received. In conveyancing there is no shortage of legal services, though there are some criticisms of their cost and quality, and questions as to their necessity. Nearly all defendants who are charged with serious crimes who appear before the Crown Court have legal aid for representation. There are criticisms of the adequacy of this service, but there is no doubt that it is generally available. *But in other areas*, even allowing for the improvements in legal aid which took effect in April 1979, *legal services are seriously inadequate*.[36] [Author's italics]

For a Royal Commission to conclude that in all areas of individual, non-commercial legal need, only house-buying and serious crime were adequately covered by the legal profession, should have led to a thorough overhaul of that profession. But neither the Royal Commission, nor the Government, nor the Law Society itself have been prepared to do that.

Part of the cause for the seriously inadequate services can be found in the administration of the Legal Aid Scheme. Solicitors submit bills for each case to the Law Society, whose officers check the figures and determine the amount to be paid, according to rates fixed by the Lord Chancellor. The system is not working well. Months and even years elapse between work on a case and receiving the fees for it. The rates allowed are well below the normal rates for private business. For instance, a solicitor can earn at least £50 per hour on conveyancing, most of which is done by a clerk; but a solicitor-advocate in the magistrates' court, who must appear in person, will be paid under the Legal Aid Scheme a maximum of £33 per hour for time in court, £27 per hour for preparatory work, and £17 per hour for travelling and waiting for the case to start. The position with advice work, and with civil cases in the county court, is little better. With High Court work there is a statutory deduction of 10 per cent from all solicitors' and barristers' legal aid fees. Legal aid is still regarded by the authorities as a rather charitable service which solicitors should subsidize out of better-paid private work. In recent years the rates have been deliberately reduced in real terms by allowing increases well below the rate of inflation. In November 1985 one well-known firm, which provided a high-quality legal aid service, had to close down its operations because they were not economically viable.

The Law Society also has responsibility for the vocational education of solicitors. Here too the emphasis on acting for the world of business and wealth is clear. Their course is divided into four heads. Head A is entitled 'The Solicitor and His [sic] Practice', which is about running a partnership and keeping accounts. Head B is 'The Solicitor and His Business Client'. Head C, 'The Solicitor and His Private Client', has three subdivisions: the conveyancing of property, the administration of wills and estates, and family and consumer law. Head D is about litigation. Considering that the course follows the narrow law degree course described earlier, it is perhaps not surprising that the majority of solicitors emerge from their training with little inclination or ability to handle work for ordinary people on legal aid.

There has nevertheless emerged over the last ten years a growing minority of solicitors who consider themselves to be people's lawyers. They work both in law centres and private firms. They are involved in securing and enforcing people's rights in the most fundamental areas of their lives: their work, their home, their family, their nationality, their personal freedom. Through the work of the Legal Action Group and other organizations, they have succeeded in learning subjects which the College of Law never taught them. Through representative bodies, such as the Law Centres' Federation and the Legal Aid Practitioners' Group, they are making demands upon the authorities to be able to serve the public under reasonable and secure conditions.

What should the response of government be? A government cannot quickly change attitudes across a whole profession, but it has a responsibility to ensure that people have access to justice. It should positively create conditions which will further that aim, not wait hopefully for the legal profession to put itself in order.

Fortunately, the two central planks of a comprehensive service are already in place. First, there are community law centres in many places which have the capacity to tackle the kind of group injustices which the private profession could never hope to redress. In the next chapter, I propose that they should be developed into a nationwide, centrally funded network.

Second, there is the Legal Aid Scheme which, in spite of weaknesses, remains a sound basis for providing advice and representation to individuals. Law centres do not seek to take on a mass of individual casework, nor should they. Private solicitors are a complementary part of any programme to secure access to justice. Their independence is of major importance, particularly in periods of right-wing government when public services are under attack. The best of them provide a service to the client which in many cases the law centres could not match; for example, nearly all of the major victories of people wrongly accused in criminal trials have been won through the work of private solicitors.

Some writers have proposed a third kind of service, of salaried solicitors employed by a centrally-funded body such as a Legal Services Commission, forming a national legal service along the lines of the National Health Service. I would reject this, at least until a network of law centres is in place. Law centres managed by local people are the first priority; while a case can be made for other forms of salaried service as well, the danger is that it would be a second-best arrangement, lacking both the local accountability of the law centre and the independence of the private solicitor.

The Legal Aid Scheme should be thoroughly overhauled.

At present a solicitor who chooses to have a full-time legal aid practice faces a number of obstacles. The aim of a thorough overhaul must be to remove the obstacles to an efficient public service while maintaining controls against abuse by solicitors looking for easy money. There would be many matters of detail to be studied, but the priority targets would be:

– to secure rates of remuneration which make it practicable for solicitors to work full-time on legal aid – perhaps with an independent review body to fix reasonable rates;

– to overcome the delays in getting paid, particularly through better systems of payments on account;

– to abolish the 10 per cent deduction for High Court fees.

There are many who advocate taking the administration of legal aid out of the hands of the Law Society entirely. It is certainly strange that the body which represents the interests of solicitors should be responsible for distributing large sums of government money to its own members. In the long term it may be logical for the Ministry of Justice to administer legal aid; in the short term the problem is not so much who runs the Legal Aid Scheme, but how it can be funded and made to work for the public.

The gaps in the coverage of the Legal Aid Scheme should be closed.

Legal aid is available for actions in the courts (but not if you are suing for libel) but not for claims before a tribunal (except the Mental Health Review Tribunal). But tribunals deal often with issues which are just as important as those in the courts. For instance, you can get legal aid to apply for bail in the magistrates' court if you are locked up as a suspected criminal, but not to apply for bail to an immigration adjudicator if locked up as a suspected illegal immigrant. If a relative dies you may get legal aid to claim damages, but not to be represented at the inquest.

The areas of greatest injustice, where people may be in desperate need of legal help but cannot get legal aid, are:

Inquests. For all their defects, inquests provide an essential forum for the investigation of unexplained deaths. The public authorities, whose conduct may have caused the death, are invariably represented by a team of lawyers. The family of the deceased, on top of the agony of their bereavement, are denied the possibility of legal aid.

Defamation actions. Legal aid is not allowed for libel and slander actions, as if the reputations of people without wealth did not matter. But when lies are printed it does matter, and it causes enormous outrage to the person who is lied about. Lawyers frequently have to advise against suing a powerful newspaper because of the prohibitive costs which would be involved.

Immigration appeals. People who are refused admission to Britain, or permission to extend their stay, have a right to appeal first to an adjudicator, and then on legal points to the Immigration Appeal Tribunal. Their decisions affect fundamental aspects of people's lives. The rules are intricate, and often there are language barriers. Yet no legal aid is available except through UKIAS, the immigrants' advisory service funded by the Home

Office. This is not enough; however well UKIAS does its work, people should have the lawyer of their choice in cases of such importance.

Social security and pensions. There is a network of tribunals concerned with benefits which are the livelihood of those who are entitled to them: supplementary benefit, national insurance, pensions. Appeals on points of law go from the tribunals to the Social Security Commissioners, whose interpretation of complex laws and regulations may affect thousands of claimants. There is no provision for legal aid.

Industrial tribunals. These deal with unfair dismissal, redundancy, discrimination in employment on grounds of race or sex, and other employment rights. Trade unionists will normally obtain representation through their union. But workers who are not in a union are often the most exploited, the worst paid, and the most in need of legal aid when they are dismissed.

In 1984 the Lord Chancellor's Advisory Committee on Legal Aid expressed itself in strong terms about the lack of legal aid in tribunals: 'There is a need to set up a full system of tribunal assistance now. The need is clearly shown by the research. The failure to act in response to our earlier Reports has had its price: people's rights have gone unenforced, their cases unheard.'[37] The Committee proposed a system of government assistance which combined two elements. First, funding should be granted to 'resource lawyers', that is, lawyers working in Citizens' Advice Bureaux, Welfare Rights Units and other independent agencies, who would train and give support to volunteer representatives. Second, legal aid for representation by a lawyer should be granted in matters of particular importance, such as test cases and cases where a person's liberty or job were at stake. The Council on Tribunals has supported these proposals, but yet again they have fallen on the Lord Chancellor's deaf ear.

**The Minister of Justice should require
training programmes which ensure that those who
undertake legal aid work have the necessary expertise.**

A solicitor who has been admitted, after the education and training described earlier, is allowed to take on any kind of legal aid work. Solicitors can claim large amounts of legal aid money, without having to submit any evidence that they are competent or experienced in the relevant area of work. Many are incompetent and inexperienced, but the public has no means of knowing.

Some tentative steps are being made to ensure that those who are paid by the State for particular kinds of work have adequate expertise. When legal aid was extended recently to certain mental health and child care cases, panels were established of solicitors who could show that they were capable in those fields of law, through proven experience or attendance at a training course. In 1984 the 'duty solicitor' scheme, through which solicitors attend on a rota at magistrates' courts and represent those who need them, was put on to a statutory basis; and a further scheme is starting to operate to advise people held in police stations. The schemes are open to solicitors who have been in regular practice in criminal defence work for the previous eighteen months.

These schemes could prove to be a welcome development in providing legal help when people are in acute need of it, provided that there are experienced solicitors on the rotas. The danger is well illustrated by a murder case tried at the Old Bailey in 1985. A Vietnamese man made a detailed 'confession' to a murder which he had not committed, in the presence of the police and the duty solicitor. The solicitor had never thought of insisting on a private interview to discover whether his client really wanted to make the confession, or whether – as emerged at the trial – he was motivated by threats from the police that his family would be deported.

The steps taken so far involve solicitors making applications to committees of lawyers, who decide whether they should join the scheme. But much more needs to be done, with the participation of the Minister of Justice, to encourage genuine specialist qualifications to be attained by solicitors doing legal aid work. There should be training programmes, going far beyond the short one-day courses which are now organized by the College of Law. Solicitors should be able to study for diplomas which indicate the attainment of specialist skills. The holding of diplomas would be advertised, so that members of the public could make an informed choice. Over time the possession of relevant diplomas would be a prerequisite for taking part in the Legal Aid Scheme. Public money would be paid to those who could give the best public service.

9 Law Centres

In 1970 a group of lawyers and community workers in North Kensington set up the first neighbourhood law centre, with donations of £4,000 made by two charities. It was an area teeming with injustices, with only one solicitor who did legal aid work. It seemed so obviously right to establish a service of salaried solicitors and legal workers who would be able to devote themselves to the people's needs, choosing priorities which reflected the seriousness of the need rather than the profitability of the case. The staff of the centre would be accountable to a management committee representing local organizations and interests.

For over two years the North Kensington Neighbourhood Law Centre remained a unique experiment. Then the value of the idea became widely recognized, and plans for law centres began to be realized in many parts of the country. By the end of 1984 there were fifty-six law centres. They have taken on agencies which have been a major source of oppression and injustice: uncaring central and local government departments, slum landlords, autocratic employers. They have been able to act for groups of people suffering a common grievance. They have educated people about their legal rights. They have helped people to organize in tenants' associations and trade unions, the better to enforce their rights. In fighting their battles they have used research, publicity, negotiation, litigation and the organization of campaigns. Often they have won. In winning they have given people confidence that injustice can be confronted and overcome. They have changed the image of the lawyer. Through their work, people have begun to believe that the lawyer can be a person working for justice. Young people have begun to study and practise law as a career which is consistent with an ambition to give service to society.

The reports of law centres describe how they have tackled acute problems which lawyers ought to be involved in but rarely were. Much of their innovative work concerns large numbers of people whose cases need a group rather than an individual remedy. Here are some examples:

Plumpstead Law Centre in south-east London, working with a local tenants' association, discovered that eighty families on a council estate suffered from damp and mould growth in their houses. They proved that this was caused by structural faults for which the council was legally responsible. They took a successful summons against the council, which pleaded guilty in court to creating a 'statutory nuisance'. The council then agreed to undertake the necessary programme of repairs.

Castlemilk Law Centre in Glasgow won a test case before the Social Security Commissioners which will benefit thousands of benefit claimants living in homes which are difficult to heat. The Commissioners laid down criteria to be followed in allowing extra benefit of up to £5.20 per week. No legal aid is available before the Commissioners, so the case could not have been handled, except as a matter of charity, by a private solicitors' firm.

Hounslow Law Centre in west London took up the case of workers in petrol stations and small shops whose employers were deducting till shortages out of their pay, whether or not the shortage was their fault. This is illegal under the Truck Act of 1896 – yet the law had been virtually unused before the centre brought a successful prosecution against a petrol company.

In 1985 the Hammersmith and Fulham Law Centre was the first legal team to use the 'genetic fingerprint' blood test to prove that a client had the right to settle in Britain. Since immigration cases do not attract legal aid, the case had to be financed from the centre's own resources.

Frequently there are so many people who need help with the law that conventional methods of advice-giving cannot meet the need. Law centres have pioneered ways of helping people and their organizations to help themselves. For example:

The Coventry Legal and Income Rights Service has set up a 'benefit shop', with carefully planned 'tick-a-box' claim forms so that people can find out for themselves what benefits they are entitled to. Over 1,000 people per week have called in at the 'shop'.

The South Manchester Law Centre, faced with 4,000 inquiries on the new British Nationality Act, were quite unable to see everyone individually. So they invited each inquirer to one of a series of local meetings; gave advice on a phone-in radio programme; distributed leaflets in English and Urdu; and held training sessions for members of community groups so that they could pass on advice to others. A normal solicitors' office could not have done any of this work.

Stockton Law Centre, finding that many homeless people were coming to them with complaints about their treatment by the council, held a meeting with the council's housing department officials and negotiated a series of procedures which would ensure that the council complied with its legal duties. In this way many homeless people who have never heard of the law centre will benefit from its work.

The list of examples could fill a book: residents objecting to a dangerous urban highway at a planning inquiry; an Asian woman lawyer reaching women in desperate need who would normally never seek advice; local co-operatives and charities needing a legal constitution; emergency services at night and weekends for people detained by the police or evicted by landlords; parents dealing with social workers who have their children in care; an advice project for patients and their families at a mental hospital; education kits for young people about their legal rights. Truly, as Lord Elwyn-Jones once said, law centres reach those parts which other agencies cannot reach.

There have also been problems, as one would expect with a new kind of organization. Staff turnover has been high, with many lawyers leaving for private practice after a few years in law centres. Pay and working conditions have often been poor. Professional standards have sometimes been below the best. The concept of community management has been difficult to put into practice, particularly in areas which do not have strong community organizations.

But the overall picture is a success story. Law centres have proved their worth throughout the legal world. The Royal Commission on Legal Services stated:

The impact of Law Centres has been out of all proportion to their size, to the number of lawyers who work in them, and to the amount of work it is possible for them to undertake. The volume of work they have attracted shows how deep is the need which they are attempting to meet.[38]

The Royal Commission quoted evidence of the Lord Chancellor's Advisory Committee on Legal Aid as being a summary of informed opinion: 'We think that law centres are, and should be, here to stay and that they are making a vital contribution to legal services.' A pamphlet of the Society of Conservative Lawyers has called for law centres to be expanded in number and put on a permanent and central financial footing. The members of the public who have used law centres, it says, 'have received a generally excellent service at a modest cost to the public purse'.[39]

After initially viewing each other with distrust, law centres and private solicitors have come to recognize that their work is complementary rather than competitive. Law centres are selective in their areas of work, trying to concentrate on the worst injustices or on test cases which will benefit a whole group. They need to refer on many individual cases to solicitors in private practice. Solicitors in turn have collaborated in duty solicitor schemes and other projects which law centres have helped to initiate.

This collaboration has taken on a more organized and constructive shape in some areas of the country through the formation of regional legal service committees. In these committees are a variety of people, from the courts, the legal profession, the law centres, the Citizens' Advice Bureaux and the organizations which represent those who suffer injustice, who come together and examine the priority needs in their area.

The pioneer venture has been the North Western Legal Services Committee, based in Manchester. With a small staff funded by the Law Society, it has been responsible for several important projects. It has established duty solicitor schemes in all the Greater Manchester magistrates' courts, so that people coming before the court can get immediate advice and representation. It has started an experimental duty solicitor scheme at Strangeways Prison, to tackle the desperate need of many prisoners for legal advice and assistance. It has promoted the teaching of law in schools, so that young people can become aware of their legal rights and responsibilities. It has put on training courses for solicitors and advice workers in vital areas of law such as mental health and immigration. It has organized an accident leaflet scheme to give guidance to the victims of accidents. It has undertaken research into the reasons for delays in magistrates' courts and how they could be avoided. As a trail-blazing organization it has the same exemplary qualities as the first law centre.

Yet the response of the government to this new movement of law centres and other organizations has been patchy and often discreditable. In 1975 Lord Chancellor Elwyn-Jones rescued five law centres which were in danger of closing, by giving grant-aid from his department's funds. But his successor, Lord

Hailsham, has failed to develop any coherent funding policy. As a result the funding of law centres is in a serious mess. Some have been funded by the Department of Environment under the Urban Programme; their initial grants are about to expire, and are not likely to be renewed. Others have been funded by the Greater London Council and the metropolitan councils, now abolished. Others have local authority funding which is severely squeezed by rate-capping. Some council-funded law centres have been axed following a change in political control.

In the north-east of England a legal services committee has been meeting for over two years. It is a region of particularly acute legal need. The committee put forward a request to the Lord Chancellor's Department for funding for a full-time secretary. The request was rejected, causing a serious loss of morale to those who had been working on the project. It seemed that the Lord Chancellor simply did not care. In May 1985, there was a debate on law centres in the House of Lords; the Lord Chancellor sat silent on the Woolsack while a junior government spokesman read a speech saying that nothing more would be done.[40]

Since the Legal Aid and Advice Act was passed in 1949, the Lord Chancellor has had the benefit of advice from the Advisory Committee on Legal Aid, a committee composed of lawyers and non-lawyers which reports every year on the state of the provision of legal services. In recent years it has been recording its increasing dismay at the failure of the Lord Chancellor to meet his responsibilities. In its report published in January 1985 the Committee referred to the 'chronic problem' caused by lack of clear ministerial direction. The Chairman of the Committee summarized the position in terms which left no room for doubt about the urgency of the need for action:

The Government's response to the Report of the Royal Commission on Legal Services did little to assuage fears about the lack of a concerted strategy for the provision of legal services. Law centres remain in limbo; the need for tribunal assistance is accepted in theory but must await the release of new resources; and the role of regional legal services committees is acknowledged but funding for the North East Legal Services Committee has been denied. Meanwhile, the local sources of funding for existing legal services have come under serious threat – through the proposed abolition of some of the local authorities that provide the funding, through the rate-capping of local authorities generally and through changes in Urban Programme policy.

Responsibility for the administration of justice – including the provision of legal aid and advice as part of the administration of justice – is already accepted by central government. It is essential that central government take the responsibility also for the many other agencies which complement, supplement, and are sometimes direct substitutes for the legal aid system, if its overall responsibility is to be met.[41]

The Minister of Justice should fund a network of community law centres throughout the country.

Whether people have access to legal help is such a fundamental issue that it should not depend on the chance of living within the boundaries of a local council which is prepared to fund a law centre. The basic funding of law centres should be taken out of the present insecurity and confusion and become the responsibility of the Minister of Justice. Over and above the government grant, local authorities would still be able to give additional funds, for instance by financing particular law centre projects.

There is a danger that centralization of funding could lead to rigid bureaucratic control. The Royal Commission paraded a horrible proposal for a 'central agency for citizens' law centres' which was to 'manage' the law centres. It expressed contempt for the concept of local management by a representative committee:

We do not think it right for people who have no knowledge of the law or the handling of legal problems and possibly little experience of managing an office, to be expected to assume direct responsibility for the professional work of a citizens' law centre.[42]

This attitude could be the death of law centres; but fortunately Lord Elwyn-Jones had already insisted, in guidelines which he laid down when Lord Chancellor, that: 'A law centre shall be under the control of a management committee the majority of whose members should normally represent the interests of the recipients of the law centre's services.' That should remain a key principle: law centres should emerge from the initiative of a community, not be imposed upon it.

The Law Centres' Federation has produced a 'design brief' for a national funding policy. It aims for a hundred law centres by 1990, and ultimately for around 10 per cent of the government's legal aid budget to be directed to law centres, which would be set up in every area where the demand can be demonstrated by a bona fide independent local steering group. It is a reasonable target.

It needs only a strong financial commitment by Government to trigger off a range of law centre projects. There are twenty-five embryo law centres whose committees are recognized by the Law Centres' Federation as observers. There is work being done to promote mobile services in rural areas, where many people have no ready access to legal help. The Federation itself has developed as a highly responsible body, carrying out training projects, advising on new technology, giving essential support to existing and potential centres; it too would be included in the funding programme.

The method of funding should be by direct grant from the Ministry of Justice to the law centres, subject to the usual requirements as to the submission of proper accounts. This would depart from a proposal made by many groups that a Legal Services Commission should be set up as a body independent of the government, receiving government funds and allocating them to law centres and other agencies. For instance the Legal Action Group claimed in its evidence to the Royal Commission:

The [Legal Services] Commission as an independent body would act as a buttress against the risk of direct intervention by the Government in the administration of legal services. Its existence would make the provision of legal services less susceptible to political changes.

Although I approved this when I helped draft that evidence, I am now far less sure. A Legal Services Commission would be a non-elected 'quango', taking important decisions without being accountable for them. If its actions were criticized – for example, if it refused funding to a law centre – the Minister would be powerless to intervene. On the other hand a Minister of Justice who was determined to cut spending could lop the Commission's grant, leaving the Commission to take responsibility for the consequent cuts. Mrs Thatcher's administration has shown that there are no 'buttresses' against the intervention of an axe-wielding government. Controversies about the funding of law centres will inevitably occur; they can best be resolved through the direct accountability of a minister to Parliament.

The Minister of Justice should fund regional legal services committees to research local needs and stimulate local initiatives.

A Minister of Justice with expanded responsibilities and spending powers would need to obtain advice and information about the needs of people around the country. The proposals in this book could not be carried out effectively by a ministry based in London without the active involvement of local people.

The North Western Regional Legal Services Committee has shown that people concerned about justice can come together constructively and launch new initiatives, even with limited funds. Similar committees should be encouraged around the country, with funding provided for administration and research.

There would then be organizations at national, regional and local levels, each independent of the Minister of Justice, but each able to feed ideas to the minister and the public about the services and reforms which are needed:

– At the national level, the Advisory Committee on Legal Aid would continue its present work. It has functioned effectively as an advocate for better legal services, even though its only right is to advise and recommend. Its membership should be broadened by requiring a majority of non-lawyers, instead of the present five lay people and eight legal. Its funding, at present a mere £34,000 a year, should be increased, in particular to allow it to undertake research.

– At the regional level, the legal services committees would bring together a range of concerned individuals and organizations, again with a majority of non-lawyers. Regional offices of the Ministry of Justice would work closely with such committees, but would not appoint or control them.

– At the community level, the network of law centres, managed by committees of local people, would be in touch with people at the grass roots.

Through the proposals in this and the previous chapter, an integrated legal services programme can be built, with independent private solicitors, community law centres, and regional committees playing complementary roles. In addition there are national agencies, such as the Child Poverty Action Group and the Children's Legal Centre, providing expertise in specialist fields, which must be given the funding, and also the rights of audience in court, to enable them to speak for the mass of people affected by government laws or judicial decisions.

All the components of the programme are already in existence, at least in a partial or experimental form. They have been shown to work. What is needed is the political will to realize their great potential for securing justice for the people of Britain.

10 Police

There can be no justice in a society which is controlled by the police. Everything else recommended in this book will be futile if the police use the force which they possess to ignore or abuse the law. For the police, unlike any other body of people except the armed forces, have the physical means to impose their will on society. They have access to offensive weapons which it would be illegal for the rest of us to carry – truncheons, guns, plastic bullets, C S gas; and to an array of expensive and largely secret technology – radio communications, bugging devices and the storage of massive amounts of computerized material. Above all they have direct powers over the lives of individuals: to lock them up, search them and their homes, fingerprint them, interrogate them – powers which, even if used correctly, are humiliating and frightening for the person involved.

There are good reasons why coercive powers have been given to the police. To be a victim of crime, above all against one's person or one's home, is also a humiliating and frightening experience, and we expect the police to be active in arresting the perpetrator. Indeed, complaints about the police are not simply about the abuse, but about the non-use, of their powers. In response to many forms of violent crime, against women and against Asians in particular, the police shrug their shoulders and claim that there is nothing to be done.

So the issue for a just society is not whether the police should have the basic powers of arresting, searching, patrolling and keeping information, but how those powers can be controlled.

Controlling the police should involve measures of two kinds:

– *Legal controls*: The powers of the police in dealing with any individual citizen must be limited to what is necessary and subject to effective safeguards against abuse.

– *Democratic controls*: The policies of the police, their priorities in law enforcement, the weapons and resources available to them, and their treatment of the community in general, must be determined by an elected body and not left to the dictate of a Chief Constable.

The legal controls have been dangerously weakened in recent years. Before 1974 the law required that every suspect who was under arrest had to be brought before a magistrates' court 'as soon as practicable', or else released. Though the wording of the law was imprecise, its intention was clear: that no one should be held in a police station for longer than the time needed to process the formalities and bring the arrested person before the next available court. This would normally involve a maximum detention of twenty-four hours or forty-eight hours at the weekend.

In practice the law was grossly abused. Police officers frequently held suspects for three or four days before bringing them to court. In London alone over a period of three months in 1979, 212 were detained for over seventy-two hours.[43] But Parliament, instead of tightening up the law to prevent abuse, has legitimized the abuse by allowing much longer legal periods of detention. In 1974 the Prevention of Terrorism Act, passed in a rush in the wake of the Birmingham bombings, authorized detention without charge for up to seven days for those suspected of 'terrorist' offences. And in 1984 the Police and Criminal Evidence Act introduced a power of detention without charge for up to ninety-six hours, subject to a warrant being granted by a magistrate. The ninety-six-hour provision is limited to 'serious' offences, but the definition of 'serious' is so loose as to include any offence which the police say is serious. For example, an offence is serious if it involves 'serious financial loss'; and the Act provides that a loss is serious 'if, having regard to all the circumstances it is serious for the person who suffers it.'[44] The purpose of these extended detention powers is to allow the police to interrogate people. Instead of obtaining objective evidence, police officers are increasingly relying on obtaining a 'confession'. The lessons of the Confait case, in which a young man confessed to a murder which he did not commit, have been ignored.

During an inquiry into policing in Wales, vivid evidence was given by one witness of the pressures which can operate on a young and vulnerable person in a police station:

I just wanted to get out of there really – the offer of bail they kept making all the time. I didn't even, as I was signing the confession statements admitting all, I didn't even then think they were going to put me in prison or anything. I thought this is all going to be very nasty in the future, but if I can get out now I can sort it out, and it was an easy way out. At that time I had been shut up for fifteen-odd hours or something, and I was totally shattered, and I didn't know where the hell I was, or what I was doing, and I just agreed . . . I had no one there with me on my side . . . I was totally in their power.'[45]

Out on the street the 1984 Act gave extended powers to stop and search members of the public. The police may stop and search if they have 'reasonable suspicion' that a person is carrying drugs, or stolen goods, or 'prohibited articles', which means anything that is intended to be used for causing injury or stealing. What constitutes 'reasonable suspicion'? Some answers were given to this by London policemen in the presence of a researcher from the Policy Studies Institute:

How does an experienced policeman decide who to stop? Well, the one that you stop is often wearing a woolly hat, he is dark in complexion, he has thick lips and he usually has dark fuzzy hair.

If I saw a black man walking down Wimbledon High Street I would definitely stop him. 'Course, down here it's a common sight so there's no point.[46]

The anger caused by such abuses of power can well be imagined. The Brixton riots of Easter 1981 were directly sparked off by an incident in which officers insisted on a provocative and unjustified search in the street. This followed the notorious 'Swamp 81' operation, in which 943 people were stopped and searched in Brixton in the course of a single week.

The democratic controls over the police are feeble in the extreme. Before 1964 the police in the cities were directly responsible to 'watch committees' composed of local councillors, who had powers of appointment and discipline over all members of the force. The counties had a different structure: their committees were composed half of magistrates and half of local councillors, and the Chief Constable had direct control over the recruitment and discipline of the officers.

In 1964, following the report of a Royal Commission, the watch committees were ended. The 'police authorities' which were then set up are composed of two-thirds local councillors, one-third magistrates. They are responsible for securing 'the maintenance of an adequate and efficient police force', while the Chief Constable has responsibility for the 'direction and control' of the force. In practice this means that Chief Constables can ignore the recommendations and advice of the police authority, and they frequently do. A police authority member put the matter succinctly to the inquiry in Wales:

The Chief Constable is a totally arbitrary power, more accountable to government ministers than to a police authority, and the extent to which the police authority can have any effect whatsoever is completely dependent upon the extent to which the Chief Constable wishes to co-operate.[47]

In London there has never been an elected police authority. The police authority for London is the Home Secretary. It is beyond my understanding to know how the vast Metropolitan Police Force can be accountable in an effective sense to a minister who has other huge national responsibilities. In practice it is not. People with grievances have no authority to which to bring them. After the disastrous police action in Southall in April 1979, in which Blair Peach died, it was left to an unofficial inquiry set up by the National Council for Civil Liberties to make cogent and devastating criticisms of the police. The Home Secretary had exonerated them entirely. In Brixton in the late 1970s feelings of anger about harassment and violence from the police had been boiling up in the black community, and the local council had set up its own inquiry chaired by a Queen's Counsel. A police authority which understood the grievances and acted to resolve them could have averted the riots of 1981.

The same anger erupted again in 1985 in Brixton and Tottenham. Again the riots were sparked by bungled, if not brutal, police operations: the shooting of Mrs Groce and the search of Mrs Jarrett's home which precipitated the debate. Again the only response of the police and the Government was to threaten more force, more weapons, more repression. If there is no redress for the bitter complaints of black people against the police, riots are certain to recur.

Over the past fifteen years, new forms of policing have been developed by the police, without a semblance of democratic approval or debate. In 1972 the National Reporting Centre was set up at Scotland Yard. Few people knew about it until 1984, when it masterminded the deployment of police forces during the miners' strike. In theory it was only co-ordinating mutual support between different police forces. In practice it became, at least in experimental form, a national police command – without being accountable to anyone, for neither the Home Secretary nor anyone else had legal powers to direct the Chief Constable who was in charge of the Centre.

The National Reporting Centre had at its disposal a total of 13,500 police officers, organized in 'police support units' from each of the forty-three police forces in England and Wales.

These units have become Britain's riot police – highly trained squads which can be mobilized for major operations around the country. We do not have a 'third force' in name like the French CRS, but we have one in fact. At Orgreave on 18 June 1984 it was able to carry out a huge quasi-military operation, with organized baton charges, backed up by horses and dogs, against totally unarmed and unprotected miners. They were carrying out manoeuvres contained in a secret manual prepared by the Association of Chief Police Officers – the Chief Constables' Club.

While legal and democratic controls over the police grow weaker, the evidence of misconduct by the police grows stronger. Those who draw attention to the misconduct of the police are smeared as being against the police in general, and thus on the side of the criminal. We are not; but we are against racist police, violent police, corrupt police. Allegations of racism, violence and corruption in the police have been constantly made over the past fifteen years, and as constantly dismissed by those in authority. But when an independent research body of high repute, the Policy Studies Institute, published the results of its day-by-day monitoring of the Metropolitan Police, then surely some understanding of the sickness within that force must have registered. The Policy Studies Institute researchers documented the most outrageous expressions of racism and sexism, and the breaking of rules, as being not exceptional but commonplace. These quotations are from the part of their report dealing with race:

Our first impression after being attached to groups of police officers in areas having a substantial ethnic minority population was that racialist language and racial prejudice were *prominent and pervasive* and that many individual officers and also whole groups were *preoccupied with ethnic differences* ... On the whole, our further research confirmed these initial impressions. [Author's italics]

In some cases senior officers undoubtedly overlooked racialism or racial prejudice when it was manifest, or participated in racialist talk themselves. It was a Chief Inspector who (in the aftermath of the Black People's Day of Action) worked himself up into a frenzy against black people and orchestrated a session of absurd racialist talk with a large group of P Cs in the canteen.[48]

In the light of that research it is not hard to believe the report of a journalist who witnessed the Tottenham riot:

A black couple trying to leave the area via Willan Road were turned back at the police lines, to a chorus of the monkey noises used to abuse black footballers by racists at soccer matches. 'Fuck off, niggers,' yelled one of the policemen. 'Go and live in the zoo. You can burn that down.' 'Get back in your rat hole, vermin,' echoed another. 'We'll be in to get you soon enough.'[49]

Legal Controls

There has recently been a huge legislative overhaul of police powers. The Police and Criminal Evidence Act and the Codes of Practice which go with it cover every aspect of policing: stop and search powers, the search of homes, powers of arrest, detention and questioning. All sorts of new forms have been issued to the police for them to fill in whenever a power is exercised.

A new government will have to study exactly how the Act has worked in practice. It requires records and statistics to be kept so that important questions can be answered, such as: how many people have been stopped and searched, and with what results; how many roadblocks have been set up, and why; how many homes have been searched under the new judges' warrants which allow the homes of innocent people to be searched for evidence; how many intimate body searches have been carried out in police stations; how many ten-year-olds have been forcibly fingerprinted; how many people have been detained for ninety-six hours; and so on.

Experience in the exercise of these powers is likely to prove that the opponents of the Act were right, and that the Act has caused an unacceptable shift of the balance of power, towards the police and against the liberty of the individual. The balance may shift still further as a result of the Public Order Bill introduced in November 1985, giving dictatorial powers to the police to control pickets and demonstrations, and creating new and vague offences. This book cannot deal with all the changes which will be needed to redress the balance. But there are three reforms which must be highlighted as fundamental.

Everyone detained in a police station must have the right to the assistance of a lawyer.

Here is another notorious example of the contrast between myth and reality in our legal system. The theory used to be expressed in a 'principle' spelled out in the preamble to the Judges' Rules – the rules laid down at a meeting of all the judges, which police officers were obliged to obey:

> Every person at any stage of an investigation should be able to communicate and to consult privately with a solicitor. This is so even if he is in custody, provided in such a case no unreasonable delay or hindrance is caused to the processes of investigation or the administration of justice by his doing so.

Home Office directions appended to the Rules stated that people in custody should be informed of their rights, both orally and by notices in the police station.

In practice police officers conducting investigations uniformly refused access by a lawyer to a suspect. As for the rule that suspects should be told of their rights, a Deputy Assistant Commissioner of the Metropolitan Police, giving evidence to the Confait inquiry, was at least truthful: 'All I can say in all honesty is that if there is a duty to inform every person in custody orally that he has a right to consult a solicitor before we commence the interview, then in practice we do not do it.'[50] Suspects who ask for solicitors are scoffed at, and the officers will later deny that they asked at all. Solicitors who go directly to the police station at the request of a relative are commonly told that the suspect does not want a solicitor, or that access is refused 'because it would hinder my inquiries'.

The 1984 Act replaces the Judges' Rules with a new provision which is unlikely to change this pattern. After stating that a person arrested and held in custody in a police station 'shall be entitled, if he so requests, to consult a solicitor privately at any time', the Act goes on to permit a senior officer, in the case of a 'serious' offence, to 'delay' the exercise of the right for up to thirty-six hours 'where he has reasonable grounds for believing' that seeing a solicitor will 'lead to interference with or harm to evidence connected with a serious arrestable offence', or have certain other consequences. The Act's criteria for preventing access to a solicitor are less vague than before, but they still depend on what a police officer believes to be reasonable, and they are equally capable of abuse.

Why should there not be an absolute right for a suspect to see a lawyer? During the debates in Parliament, ministers constructed scenarios in which solicitors might be asked to pass on what seemed to be an innocent message to the suspect's wife, but was really a coded instruction to an accomplice. It was unbelievably far-fetched. The reality was that the police wanted to have enough time to browbeat suspects into a confession without a solicitor getting in the way.

The absolute right of a suspect to see a lawyer would be coupled to the duty solicitor scheme of lawyers able to attend police stations on a round-the-clock rota. Such a scheme has already been launched; it is a major step forward in making lawyers available where they are most needed. The combination of the right to see a solicitor, and the availability of independent solicitors on the spot, would provide a real chance of avoiding the terrible injustice of a false confession. Any breach of the right should automatically result in the exclusion of the 'confession' from being used in evidence.

All interviews with suspects should be tape-recorded.

The police have been keen to use modern technology in the detection of crime, much less so in the protection of the suspect from unfair questions or fabricated interviews. Tape-recording was accepted in principle by the Home Secretary in November 1981. A year later it was announced that two years of 'field trials' would be started, and they began in the following year in six areas. There is still no national scheme in prospect.

In the 1984 Act it was written into the law for the first time that a person may be detained for questioning. Yet nothing has been done to ensure that the record of such questioning is a true one. It is still possible for police officers to compose 'verbals' after a long interview – that is, a supposed word-for-word account of the interview, written up afterwards, and not shown to the suspect until months later when it becomes part of the evidence at his or her trial. At best this 'recollection' of an interview will be biased and inaccurate, at worst a complete fabrication to bolster up a weak case. It is a disgraceful part of our system of justice, and quite unnecessary, since modern machinery can guarantee an accurate record.

The Prevention of Terrorism Act should be repealed.

Between 1974 and 1984, 5,905 people were detained under the 'temporary' legislation which authorized the detention of people incommunicado for up to seven days. 5,155 were released without a charge or any other action against them. Only 344 were eventually found guilty of an offence, of which 97 were sentenced to more than one year's imprisonment. The sweeping powers of the Act have caused great suffering to thousands of people and their relatives, for the sake of less than one hundred convictions for serious crimes. When one remembers that ordinary powers of arrest are available in any case for all serious crimes, why must these 'emergency' laws be continued?

The Act also gives powers to the Home Secretary to exclude people from entering a part of their country. People in Northern Ireland may be excluded from Great Britain, and vice versa. It is ironic that this is done in order to maintain the unity of Britain and Northern Ireland. 310 people have been excluded from Great Britain and in one case, that of Mr and Mrs McLoughlin, the husband is excluded from Northern Ireland and the wife is excluded from Great Britain. Although British citizens, they cannot live together in any part of their country, and are now refugees in the Republic of Ireland.

The Act operates as a powerful obstacle to free communication with people from Northern Ireland, who have frequently been turned back or detained when invited to speak at meetings; for example, I recall trying in vain to secure the release of Ann Boyle and Maire O'Hare, who were detained for five days after arriving to address the Socialist Feminine Conference in London in 1979. It was sheer harassment; it emerged later that they were not questioned about anything specific. But the High Court, when an application for habeas corpus was made, said that it was powerless to intervene.

The Act was widened in 1984 to include the right to detain those suspected of acts of 'terrorism', which is defined as 'the use of violence for political ends', committed in any part of the world. Anyone involved in a liberation movement against a dictatorial regime could fall within the definition.

It is time to bring these 'temporary' measures to an end. They are much more powerful as a weapon of political harassment than as a means of detecting crime. Those who are genuinely suspected of using violence, whether for political ends or not, can be legally arrested under the ordinary law, and under the 1984 Act detained for ninety-six hours. There is no need for more repressive laws.

Democratic Controls

Police authorities should be given power to determine policing policies and should have ultimate responsibility for police actions.

There is no substitute for democracy as an effective means of controlling the exercise of power. If you look at any other public service – the hospitals, the schools, the social services, the fire brigade, the protection of environmental health – you will find that in overall charge is a committee of elected people. In each case the professional management take the day-to-day decisions about particular cases. But they do not have untrammelled power. Above them are people who are conscious that they can be voted out of office if they mismanage the services which they control.

Such democratic machinery is far from perfect, but it is infinitely better than no machinery at all. The present police authorities do not have any control over the policies or operations of their forces. They are at best an advisory committee. Their relationship with their Chief Constable is quite different from the relationship of, for instance, a Social Services Committee to its Director of Social Services. The Director acts in the name of the council and is accountable to the council. The Committee, having listened to the professional advice of the Director, takes decisions on resources, policies and priorities. When a disaster happens, such as the death by battering of a child in care, the council must carry the responsibility of finding out what went wrong.

But in the case of policing, which impinges far more on the community than social work, it is the Chief Constable who has the first and last word. The representatives of the community have no legal responsibility for police operations, and their ideas can be treated with contempt. For example, after the riots in Toxteth the Merseyside Police Authority did its utmost to discover the grievances which had caused the riots and to elaborate policies which would provide remedies. It met with constant obstruction from a Chief Constable who thought he knew better.

Why should this be so? Leon Brittan on behalf of the Home Office defended the position in these terms:

I have emphasized that Chief Constables are operationally independent. The Home Secretary cannot give them instructions . . . about the deployment of their officers. Nor may a police authority issue such instructions. That is the key element in our policing arrangements. The reason is sound. It has always been true that the police must act in the name and with the support of the community as a whole. The impartiality and independence of Chief Constables in their force is therefore vital.[51]

But how can Chief Constables, many of whom are responsible for several counties, act 'in the name of the community as a whole' if there is no authority elected by the community to express its will? If the Chief Constable is to use personal intuition to interpret what 'the community as a whole' will support, it is a recipe for dictatorship.

The Police and Criminal Evidence Act requires that: 'Arrangements shall be made in each police area for obtaining the views of the people in that area about matters concerning the policing of that area and for obtaining their co-operation with the police in preventing crime in the area.' Such consultation is desirable, but it is not to be confused with accountability, for the Chief Constable can with impunity override the views of those consulted. For example, before the Southall demonstration in April 1979, local community organizations had had full consultation with the community liaison officer, Chief Inspector Gosse. But the officer in command took no notice of the agreement which had been reached, saying, 'Who the fuck's Gosse – I'm in charge here.' The National Council for Civil Liberties inquiry commented: 'The officers now in charge of the demonstration had deprived themselves of the obvious benefit to be gained from the mutual understanding between the community and the local police which had been built up over a lengthy period.'[52] Southall is a tragic example which illustrates how ludicrous it is to suppose that the police can be trusted, in the absence of any democratic supervision, to act 'in the name and with the support of the community as a whole'.

There must therefore be a change in the law. Police authorities, consisting entirely of elected members, should be the employers of the police and responsible for the overall direction of their work. Like any other public employer, they would determine the allocation of funds and the policies of the force. They would determine what resources would be put into the enforcing of which laws – a discretion which at present rests entirely with the Chief Constable. They would be able to require reports on any policing matter, provided that this would not prejudice pending police investigations into particular crimes or constitute a contempt of court.

Such a change would be of value both to the community and to the police. Ordinary people through their elected authorities would have a say in the policing of their area, and a channel through which their complaints about policing policy could be expressed. The grievances of the community would not only be about the infringement of civil liberties; they would also be about the failure of the police to deal with crime. Hard questions about resources, methods of patrolling, technology, community policing, law enforcement priorities, would be tackled collectively in open debate. Police officers, who are more and more becoming a force apart from the people, would be drawn into the debate, instead of deciding these issues in secret. Accountability should not be seen as a burden on the police, but as the only way in which they will be able, as most of them no doubt wish, to police with the consent of the community.

Some have expressed the fear that democratic control over policing would lead to hard-line policies in Conservative-controlled authorities, and thus to the persecution of unpopular minorities. Two answers need to be made to that argument. First, we already have hard-line policing, co-ordinated in secret by the Association of Chief Police Officers. Unpopular minorities are already victimized. Democratic policing, even under right-wing authorities, would allow policies at least to be exposed and challenged, and ultimately to be changed through the ballot box. Second, the way to protect unpopular minorities is not to restrict democracy, but to underpin the basic rights of everyone by laws which override all policing decisions. I turn in the final chapter to these fundamental human rights.

London must have an elected police authority.

The Metropolitan Police Force employs around 27,000 officers and 10,000 civilian staff, and receives nearly a third of all Government funds spent on the police over the whole country. In 1982–3 its budget was £727 million, of which £323 million came from the rates. Yet local councillors have no say in London's policing.

Lord Scarman, in his report on the Brixton riots, recognized the force of the demand for an elected authority, but did not recommend it, saying only that:

There are good reasons for the national accountability of the Metropolitan Police. I do not believe that Parliament would wish to see ultimate responsibility for the policing of the nation's capital transferred from a senior minister responsible to it and put in the hands of a local body, however important.[53]

Why not? Lord Scarman did not set out the 'good reasons', but they appear to relate to the various functions of national significance which the Metropolitan Police undertake, such as the protection of the Royal Family, government ministers and embassies, and services such as the Criminal Records Office, and the National Police Computer, which are at the disposal of police forces throughout the country.

It may be that some police services should remain under the control of the Home Secretary, who already has other national police functions, such as the responsibility of Her Majesty's Inspectors of Constabulary. That does not mean that the overwhelming majority of the Metropolitan Police's activities, which concern the policing of London, should not be determined by Londoners. The details of a new authority will need careful study, particularly in the aftermath of the abolition of the Greater London Council. A new GLC, or whatever strategic authority takes its place, is the appropriate body to be a police authority, for the Metropolitan Police area is only marginally greater than the boundaries of Greater London.

The problems of corruption, violence and racism in the Metropolitan Police are enormous. Operation Countryman failed to solve corruption in the CID, and publication of the Policy Studies Institute report, welcome though it is, will not of itself alter the racism of so many of London's officers. There seems to be a particular arrogance in the Metropolitan Police, a resistance to outside scrutiny, which may be the result of decades of non-accountability. The creation of an elected police authority will not solve these problems quickly, but it will give a chance, for the first time in history, for Londoners to exercise control over the way in which their city is policed.

11 Human Rights

Behind all the proposals in this book for the reform of particular agencies of the law, lie fundamental questions about the values of our society. Britain in recent years has become less free, less tolerant, less respectful of the rights of the individual. 'Freedom' under Mrs Thatcher's Government has been predominantly the freedom of those who have money to make more. Many other freedoms have been diminished.

The freedom to organize and demonstrate for better conditions of life has been chipped away by sweeping police powers and heavy police methods. The freedom to strike in defence of one's job has been cut down to a point where almost all effective action is illegal. The freedom to be a political dissenter still exists, at the risk of being watched and listened to by Special Branch as a subversive.

Indignities continue to be heaped upon people who do not fit the dominant stereotype. Women are depicted as bodies without minds in the pages of the tabloid press, reflecting the treatment received by many women in the home. The AIDS epidemic becomes an occasion not to show concern for the dying but to revile the gay community. The causes of the alienation of black people, so well identified by Lord Scarman in 1981, have been ignored by those in power.

And all the time the power of the authorities grows stronger. Through their armed forces, their nuclear bases, their secret service, their riot police, they make their plans in secret for the ordering of our lives.

The next government must turn away from secrecy and authoritarianism to be a determined champion of openness and human rights, as no government as been before. For in the post-war years, while international concern for human rights has intensified, Britain has lagged behind. In their foreign policy, British governments of every colour have supported the apartheid regime of South Africa and encouraged the most aggressive actions of the United States. In their domestic actions, they have been major violators of the European Convention on Human Rights.

The Convention was born out of a determination never again to allow the horrors of fascism to arise in Europe. Its full title reflects that ideal: the Convention for the Protection of Human Rights and Fundamental Freedoms. It provides an excellent statement of the rights which a democratic society is meant to provide. The list of rights is not complete: there is no right to a job, or to a basic income, or to a place to live in, and these omissions reflect the capitalist orientation of those who framed it. But it is strong in its expression of what people broadly understand to be their 'democratic rights', such as the rights to liberty, to due process of law, to freedom of conscience, expression and assembly.

Britain has been found guilty by the European Court in Strasbourg more often than any other country. The catalogue of cases reflects accurately those areas of British life where cruelty and bigotry often prevail over decency and tolerance:

– *Brutality in Northern Ireland*: Britain was found guilty of inhuman and degrading treatment in the interrogation of Republican prisoners.[54]

– *Corporal punishment*: Britain was condemned for the practice of judicial birching in the Isle of Man, and for beating in schools against the wishes of parents.[55]

– *Immigration policies*: The Court found that by refusing to allow foreign husbands to join their wives who were settled in Britain, while allowing foreign wives to join their husbands, the Government had violated the non-discrimination provisions of the Convention.[56]

– *Homosexuality*: The criminalization of all acts of sex between men in Northern Ireland was held to be a violation of the
right to respect for private and family life.[57]

– *Prisoners*: In a succession of judgments the Court held that
the British prison rules were incompatible with the right to
have free access to a court of law; the right to respect for one's
correspondence; and the right to marry.[58]

– *Mental patients*: Patients at Broadmoor established that
they had been denied the right to have the legality of their
detention tested in a court of law.[59]

The common thread running through these cases, which are
not the whole list of findings against Britain, is that the victims
were people without political clout. The violation of their
human rights had not been prevented by the normal political or
judicial processes. It took an international court to force a
change in British law.

A government which believed in justice would not only ensure
that the minimum norms of the European Convention were
observed; it would examine all its laws and practices, with a
view to making Britain an exemplary model in the promotion of
human rights, instead of being an exemplary offender.

The European Convention on Human Rights should be incorporated into British Law.

At present, even though Britain is a signatory to the European
Convention, the British courts may ignore it. So a Bill of Rights
needs to be enacted, obliging the courts to recognize and apply
the Convention. There are precedents in history for the writing
of positive rights into British law: Magna Carta in 1215, the Bill
of Rights in 1688. Today, in the face of modern excesses of
State power, another great declaration of the rights of the citizen
is needed.

At the present time people only have the 'liberty' to do what is not prohibited by any law. Given the multiplicity of crimes, police powers and judge-made laws, this often means that they can do very little. For example, any gathering on the pavement is illegal, however little it inconveniences other pedestrians; for, as a judge put it recently in the case of a street entertainer, 'where stopping on the highway cannot properly be said to be ancillary or part and parcel of one's right to pass and re-pass along the highway, then the obstruction becomes unreasonable, and there is an obstruction contrary to the provisions of [the Highways Act].'[60]

The passing of the Convention into British law would allow fundamental arguments about the ambit of human rights to be raised before judges and juries. In trials involving issues of free speech, such as Official Secrets Act cases, or free assembly, such as the miners' riot trials, the jury would be urged by the defence to accept that the State had violated the human rights of the accused. The 'common law' developed by the judges would be subordinated to the rights guaranteed by the Convention.

There is already a draft of a Bill of Rights before Parliament: the Human Rights and Fundamental Freedoms Bill, introduced in the House of Lords in December 1985, supported by peers of all parties, but denied Government backing. Under it, all previous laws and Acts of Parliament would need to be interpreted so as to conform with the Convention. Later Acts of Parliament would also be subject to the Convention unless Parliament specifically declared that the Convention would not apply.

Many socialists have argued against the incorporation of the Convention into British law, on the grounds that the judges would be sure to interpret it restrictively. To that there are two answers. First, as a matter of principle, it would be ridiculous to proclaim the value of an international statement of fundamental rights – which the Convention provides, even if incompletely – and yet refuse to make it part of one's own law. Second, the existence of such a statement in the law would certainly affect the way in which civil liberty issues were presented in the courts, and in time would affect the decisions of the judges themselves. It would be possible to present arguments about democratic principles, rather than about the meaning of legal rules. With growing awareness and debate by the public about their newly defined rights, the minds of the judges could be educated, and some at least of the arguments would be won by the individual against the State.

But enacting a Bill of Rights should be seen only as a first step. It is not a panacea for the evils of society. Many of the rights in the Convention are subject to exceptions which are expressed in broad terms. Article 8 is a typical example. After declaring that 'everyone has the right to respect for his private and family life, his home and his correspondence', it continues:

There shall be no interference by a public authority with the exercise of this right except such as is in accordance with the law and is necessary in a democratic society in the interests of national security, public safety or the economic well-being of the country, for the prevention of disorder or crime, for the protection of health or morals, or for the protection of the rights and freedoms of others.

The rights of freedom of speech and freedom of association are qualified in similar language. One can easily foresee how many judges will interpret them.

Accordingly the commitment to human rights must go beyond the enactment of a Bill of Rights. Specific reforms will be needed as well before many of the rights can be universally enjoyed and enforced in reality.

For example, the right to respect for private life, quoted above from Article 8, is clearly not enjoyed by those young men between sixteen and twenty-one who wish to have homosexual relations. Everyone else in their age group can develop their sexuality in free relationships, if and when they chose to do so. But young gay men, if they wish to have sexual relations, must commit a crime. Their future should not have to depend on how judges or juries might interpret Article 8. The law should be specifically amended.

The right to freedom of expression, set out in Article 10, is denied, in an often outrageous way, to government employees who may be driven by their conscience to speak to the Press. Under section 2 of the Official Secrets Act they can be prosecuted and sentenced to two years' imprisonment, even if the leaked information has no security implications. For years governments have promised to repeal section 2 and replace it with a Freedom of Information Act. But the civil service delights in secrecy, and has prevented any change in the law.

As for the right of peaceful assembly, set out in Article 11, it may scarcely survive the Public Order Bill now going through Parliament. For if the police have powers to impose conditions about the size, location and duration of a demonstration, then there is no right to assemble, only a permission to assemble – if the police agree.

The judges, in their decisions during the miners' strike and in other picketing cases, have shown little inclination to restrict the discretionary powers of the police. Here again, specific legislation will be needed.

These are only examples of the problems to be tackled by a government which resolved that human rights must come first. The whole list of necessary reforms would require a book in itself. Not only laws must be changed, but administrative practices and procedures, especially in those departments of government where conservatism and prejudice are most pervasive. The secret service, the armed forces, the immigration service, the prison department, would all need particular attention.

Justice is not only the business of lawyers and courts. The whole of society must be vigilant to ensure that the human rights of all its members are protected by just laws, respected by the agencies of the State, and capable of being enforced by fair and impartial courts. We are far away from that ideal. The powers of those who want to perpetuate injustice are massive – but they are not invincible. I have no doubt at all that if a government set its hand to the task of achieving justice, acting on the ideas and proposals in this book, the people of Britain would respond with enthusiasm. For the old promise of Magna Carta is still part of English law, and it needs again to be honoured: 'We will not deny or defer to anyone either justice or right.'

Notes

1. Lord Hailsham, The Child & Co. Lecture 1978, p. 13.
2. National Health Service Act 1946, section 1(1).
3. Advisory Committee on Legal Aid, *34th Annual Report*, January 1985, para. 402.
4. The figures for age, sex and professional background were supplied to me by the Lord Chancellor's Department. Information about school and university was taken from *Who's Who 1985*.
5. Lord Hailsham, speech to the Common Law Bar Association, *Law Society Gazette*, 28 August 1985, p. 2,335.
6. Lord Justice Scrutton, address to the University of Cambridge Law Society, 18 November 1920, *I Cambridge Law Journal*, p. 8.
7. *R. v. Mansfield Justices, ex parte Sharkey* (1985) I All E. R., p. 202.
8. J. A. G. Griffith, *The Politics of the Judiciary*, Fontana, 1977, 3rd edn, p. 233.
9. *Prison Information Bulletin*, no. 5, June 1985, p. 22.
10. Malcolm Dean, 'Serious Cases Kept Away from Lenient Judges', *Guardian*, 10 September 1984.
11. Lord Hailsham, speech at the Annual General Meeting of the Magistrates Association, 12 October 1984.
12. Central Office of Information, *Justices of the Peace in England and Wales: Their Appointment and Duties Explained*, Central Office of Information, 1984.
13. Sir Thomas Skryme, *The Changing Image of the Magistracy*, Macmillan, 1983, p. 62.
14. M. King and C. May, *Black Magistrates*, Cobden Trust, 1985, p. 105.
15. *Legal Action Group Bulletin*, November 1982, p. 12.
16. *R. v. Bingham Justices, ex parte Jowitt*, quoted in the *Magistrate*, June 1978.
17. Elizabeth Burney, *Justices of the Peace: Magistrate, Court and Community*, Hutchinson, 1979, p. 188.
18. King and May, *Black Magistrates*, p. 26.
19. Burney, *Justices of the Peace*, p. 90.
20. ibid., p. 69.
21. Labour Campaign for Criminal Justice, *The Selection and Appointment of Labour Candidates for the Magistracy: A Survey*, Labour Campaign for Criminal Justice, June 1983, p. 1.
22. King and May, *Black Magistrates*, p. 35.

23. Burney, *Justices of the Peace*, p. 69.
24. King and May, *Black Magistrates*, p. 42.
25. Employment Protection (Consolidation) Act 1978, section 29.
26. Brian Cooke, 'The Appointment of Justices of the Peace: The Advisory Committee System', *Magistrate*, vol. 40, no. 5, p. 71.
27. *R. v. McKenlay* (1979) 1 Cr. App. Rep. (S) 161.
28. H. C. Hansard, Written Answers, 14 November 1984, col. 256. There are further delays between first appearance in court and committal for trial, for which figures are not available.
29. 'What is Going On?' (by 'a methodist minister in Liverpool'), *Legal Action Group Bulletin*, April 1975, p. 94.
30. Bill Nash, '£3,500 A Year for Just Waiting', *Legal Action Group Bulletin*, October 1976, p. 222.
31. Royal Commission on Legal Services, *Final Report*, October 1979, Cmnd 648, para. 36.47.
32. A. E. Bottoms and J. D. McLean, *Defendants in the Criminal Process*, Routledge, 1976.
33. Royal Commission on Legal Services, *Final Report*, para. 33.79.
34. ibid., para. 10.11.
35. ibid., para. 36.81.
36. ibid., para. 4.21.
37. Advisory Committee on Legal Aid, *33rd Annual Report*, December 1983, para. 277.
38. Royal Commission on Legal Services, *Final Report*, para. 8.11.
39. R. B. L. Prior, *Law Centres: A Movement at a Halt*, Conservative Political Centre for the Society of Conservative Lawyers, September 1984, p. 3.
40. H. L. Hansard, 8 May 1985, col. 718.
41. Advisory Committee on Legal Aid, *34th Annual Report*, January 1985, preface, paras. 4–5; *see also* paras. 401–2.
42. Royal Commission on Legal Services, *Final Report*, para. 8.26.
43. Survey done for the Royal Commission on Criminal Procedure, cited in the Commission's Report, January 1981, para. 3.96.
44. Police and Criminal Evidence Act 1984, section 116(7).
45. John Davies, Tony Gifford and Tony Richards, *Political Policing in Wales*, Welsh Council for Civil and Political Liberties, 1984, para. 7.30.
46. Policy Studies Institute (PSI), *Police and People in London*, vol. IV, PSI Report, PSI, 1983, pp. 129–30.
47. Davies, Gifford and Richards, *Political Policing in Wales*, para. 10.11.
48. Policy Studies Institute (PSI), *Police and People in London*, vol. IV, PSI report, 1983, pp. 109, 123.
49. Steve Platt, 'The Innocence of Broadwater Estate', *New Society*, 11 October 1984, p. 48.
50. Sir Henry Fisher, *Maxwell Confait*, report, House of Commons Paper 90, HMSO, 1977, para. 17.6.
51. H. C. Hansard, 25 January 1980, col. 901.

52. *Southall 23 April 1979*, report of the unofficial committee of inquiry, Chairman Professor Michael Dummett, National Council for Civil Liberties, 1980, para. 9.26.

53. *The Brixton Disorders, April 10–12, 1981: Inquiry Report*, Chairman Lord Scarman, Cmnd 8427, HMSO 1981, para. 5.68 (published in Penguin as *The Scarman Report: The Brixton Disorders 10–12 April 1981*, 1982).

54. *Ireland* v. *United Kingdom*, European Human Rights Reports (EHRR), 1978, vol. 2, p. 25.

55. *Tyrer* v. *United Kingdom*, EHRR, 1980, vol. 3, p. 531; *Campbell and Cosans* v. *United Kingdom*, EHRR, 1978, vol. 2, p. 1.

56. *Abdulaziz, Cabales and Balkandali* v. *United Kingdom*, European Court of Human Rights (ECHR) report, 1985, Series A, no. 94.

57. *Dudgeon* v. *United Kingdom*, EHRR, 1980, vol. 3, p. 40.

58. *Golder* v. *United Kingdom*, EHRR, 1975, vol. 1, p. 524; *Silver* v. *United Kingdom*, ECHR report, 1985, Series A, no. 94. In the marriage case (*Hamer* v. *United Kingdom*) the United Kingdom Government changed its rules in 1981, so that no court ruling was needed.

59. *X* v. *United Kingdom*, ECHR report, 1981, Series A, no. 46.

60. *Waite* v. *Taylor*, 1 February 1985, Divisional Court.

Index

MORE ABOUT PENGUINS, PELICANS, PEREGRINES AND PUFFINS

For further information about books available from Penguins please write to Dept EP, Penguin Books Ltd, Harmondsworth, Middlesex UB7 0DA.

In the U.S.A.: For a complete list of books available from Penguins in the United States write to Dept DG, Penguin Books, 299 Murray Hill Parkway, East Rutherford, New Jersey 07073.

In Canada: For a complete list of books available from Penguins in Canada write to Penguin Books Canada Limited, 2801 John Street, Markham,
Ontario L3R 1B4.

In Australia: For a complete list of books available from Penguins in Australia write to the Marketing Department, Penguin Books Australia Ltd, P.O. Box 257, Ringwood, Victoria 3134.

In New Zealand: For a complete list of books available from Penguins in New Zealand write to the Marketing Department, Penguin Books (N.Z.) Ltd, Private Bag, Takapuna, Auckland 9.

In India: For a complete list of books available from Penguins in India write to Penguin Overseas Ltd, 706 Eros Apartments, 56 Nehru Place, New Delhi 110019.

A CHOICE OF
PELICANS AND PEREGRINES

☐ *A Question of Economics* **Peter Donaldson** £4.95

Twenty key issues – from the City and big business to trades unions – clarified and discussed by Peter Donaldson, author of *10 × Economics* and one of our greatest popularizers of economics.

☐ *Inside the Inner City* **Paul Harrison** £4.95

A report on urban poverty and conflict by the author of *Inside the Third World*. 'A major piece of evidence' – *Sunday Times*. 'A classic: it tells us what it is really like to be poor, and why' – *Time Out*

☐ *What Philosophy Is* **Anthony O'Hear** £4.95

What are human beings? How should people act? How do our thoughts and words relate to reality? Contemporary attitudes to these age-old questions are discussed in this new study, an eloquent and brilliant introduction to philosophy today.

☐ *The Arabs* **Peter Mansfield** £4.95

New Edition. 'Should be studied by anyone who wants to know about the Arab world and how the Arabs have become what they are today' – *Sunday Times*

☐ *Religion and the Rise of Capitalism*
R. H. Tawney £3.95

The classic study of religious thought of social and economic issues from the later middle ages to the early eighteenth century.

☐ *The Mathematical Experience*
Philip J. Davis and Reuben Hersh £7.95

Not since *Gödel, Escher, Bach* has such an entertaining book been written on the relationship of mathematics to the arts and sciences. 'It deserves to be read by everyone ... an instant classic' – *New Scientist*